Lake Como

You are holding a reproduction of an original work that is in the public domain in the United States of America, and possibly other countries. You may freely copy and distribute this work as no entity (individual or corporate) has a copyright on the body of the work. This book may contain prior copyright references, and library stamps (as most of these works were scanned from library copies). These have been scanned and retained as part of the historical artifact.

This book may have occasional imperfections such as missing or blurred pages, poor pictures, errant marks, etc. that were either part of the original artifact, or were introduced by the scanning process. We believe this work is culturally important, and despite the imperfections, have elected to bring it back into print as part of our continuing commitment to the preservation of printed works worldwide. We appreciate your understanding of the imperfections in the preservation process, and hope you enjoy this valuable book.

A World's Shrine

Como

LAKE COMO

A World's Shrine

By

Virginia W. Johnson

Author of "The Lily of the Arno," "America's Godfather," "Genoa, the Superb," "The House of the Musician," etc.

"I have brought you a little gift from my native place . . ."
PLINY, THE YOUNGER

London
Gay and Bird
22, Bedford Street, Strand
1902

Copyright, 1902,
BY A. S. BARNES & COMPANY

All rights reserved.

Published June, 1902

UNIVERSITY PRESS · JOHN WILSON
AND SON · CAMBRIDGE, U. S. A.

Contents

		Page
I.	THE FOUR GATES OF A TINY EDEN	3
II.	ACROSS THE CENTURIES	7
III.	THE COUNTRY GENTLEMAN	18
IV.	A VANISHED HOUSE	54
V.	PLINY'S ROSE	61
VI.	AT THE SPRING	70
VII.	A TEMPLE OF JUPITER	81
VIII.	SIGNAL TOWERS	90
IX.	AN ANCHORITE	95
X.	A MEDIÆVAL QUEEN	104
XI.	A TINY GIBRALTAR	111
XII.	A SPORTSMAN OF THE MIDDLE AGES	119
XIII.	SPANISH FOOTSTEPS	125
XIV.	A WITCH	140
XV.	THE MAGICIANS	149
XVI.	"ALL THE WORLD'S A STAGE"	160
XVII.	A MUSICAL MEMORY	176
XVIII.	A FISHERMAN	189
XIX.	THE HUMAN KEY-STONE	195

Contents

THE SEASONS.

I. Winter.
            Page
XX. A Patriarchal Villa 209

II. Spring.
XXI. Blossoms 219

III. Summer.
XXII. A Conceited Snail 227

IV. Autumn.
XXIII. His Own Vine and Fig-Tree . . . 239
XXIV. Boyhood 254
XXV. Tragedy in Sunshine 266
XXVI. The Winds of Como 272

Illustrations

Como	. . . .	. Frontispiece
The Cathedral of Como	. . . . .	Facing Page 14
Bellaggio	. . . .	,, 66
The Comacina	. . . .	,, 114
A Village Street	. . . .	,, 144
Home of Queen Caroline	. . . . .	,, 160
A Como Girl	. . . .	,, 242
Menaggio	. . . .	,, 280

WORTHY Pausanius is congratulated that after the lapse of some seventeen centuries his work on Greece should be read by unknown nations as a sort of classical Murray or Baedeker. Courage, painstaking compiler of even a local guidebook! Do not apologise to a critical and bored public for such labour of love, but hold up thy head, and dare to face the audience, which may prove to be future generations.

A World's Shrine

I

THE FOUR GATES OF A TINY EDEN

AFLOAT on Como! Such is the dream, at least once in a lifetime, of the most prosaic mortal. What memories the mere suggestion evokes! A sheet of crystal, set deep in the enfolding hills like a cup, this goal of summer travel possesses a charm of association for each new generation. Lake Como is a siren ever young. The sheltered haunt is unique among the inland sheets of water of the earth in a certain richness of historical association in the lapse of centuries. The finger of Time may mark the crumbling ruins of monastery and fortress on slope or promontory, but the clear, pellucid surface still reflects the passing clouds. Pilgrims of every

A World's Shrine

race thus seek these shrines. Does not the German savant muse over his pipe of the Wanderjahre of adolescence when every student, inspired by Goethe, visited Italy, and he climbed the heights of Como, light of heart and purse, to sleep at wayside inns, and gather cystus, primula, or gentian in the valleys and ravines? The grandparents in their chimney-corner, within sound of the North Sea, smile at each other in celebrating their Golden Wedding such time as the bride and bridegroom of to-day prepare their modern luggage for a journey to Bellaggio. Is not the American soothed by the souvenir of drifting idly in a boat beneath garden hedges of bay and cyprus, redolent of the terraces of jasmine, magnolia, orange, and citron beyond, in a brief expansion of freedom from the bondage of routine? Como opens her gates in welcome. On the south side the tourist quits the train which has glided through the mazes of the St. Gothard route at the town, and launches on the narrow channel wending between green hills to open spaces beyond.

The Four Gates of a Tiny Eden

Eastward Lecco lures the wayfarer from the marble silence of Venice, reflecting dome and parapet in sluggish lagoons, to the blooming freshness of the Brianza, past Castello, the pilgrim shrine of Baro, and the Val Madrera. Westward Menaggio guards the twin portal from Lugano, the realm of peaceful countryside, with beech and walnut, ripening fig and grape, spanned by a toy railway adapted to a holiday-making mood. The mountain world is sentinel of the North, where hurrying crowds descend from glacier and snow-field in the brief hours of summer to Colico and Varenna. Oh, friendly reader, avoid all other craft, from the plodding daily steamer to the lumbering *camballo*, with odd rudder and arabesque gunwale, the barge of Pliny's time, and embark in the light skiff of Memory on these tranquil waters! Follow your own whim of the moment, and adorn the shallop with such pomp of imagination as the wreath of laurel, arazzi, and pictures on the fleet of boats which celebrated the marriage of Gian Galeazzo in 1493, to make short voyages from inlet to rocky point. Pliny's own cockle-shell, with painted planks, awnings, garlands of roses, and leaves twined about the staves, may even suit better your caprice. Hoist a filmy sail of fancy, and breast the tide independent of those winds of Como, the night *Tivano* the *tramontana*, or *la Breva* of midday from the southwest. Dip the oar of reverie into the stream of Lethe in shore, where roses shed their petals on marble steps laved by the tide, and orchids spread wings of white, pink, and sulphur tints amidst the shrubbery, and hold converse with a shadowy brotherhood of past generations who have done likewise.

Years are as a day here, and the recurring seasons only change the scenes of a mimic theatre.

II

ACROSS THE CENTURIES

THAT south gate of Como, the cradle of Pliny the Younger, is neither especially picturesque in situation, nor attractive in architecture, placed as it is between the narrow strip of water and the higher level of the railway. The town has been described as resembling a crab stretched along the shore and slope. This miniature sovereign of a little world has a history out of all proportion to existing magnitude. Como may be compared to a drop of water reflecting the colours of environment.

Ancient Italian chroniclers, leisurely discursive in the treatment of history through musty volumes on library shelves, trace the settlement of Como to Comerus, the ancestor of Japeth, one hundred and thirty years after the Deluge.

A World's Shrine

Still another version is the founding of the place by a certain Antenore, who also built Padua after the destruction of Troy. A further inference is that the Etruscans in sending forth twelve colonies to build cities from the Po to the Alps, traced these boundaries as well. A first group of habitations, round in shape, constructed of interlaced branches, or reeds, with a thatched roof, expanded, in time, to a Latin colony of the date of the Roman Republic. The town, shown favour by Cæsar and Augustus, and boasting of Etruscan and Greek culture in the inhabitants, had a Forum, Gymnasium, Bath, Basilica, and Portico. Assuredly the nocturnal Triumviri of such cities were no other than the flying squadron of Carabinieri taking the beat of the suburbs of Italian towns in the nineteenth century. The theatre was already an important feature, as is the modern circus. Placards were posted about the streets vaunting the tricks of the jugglers, and inviting the public to witness the feats of acrobats in an interior perfumed with the scents of crocus and saffron essences. Traffic had

Across the Centuries

many similarities with the present day. No doubt the piercing cry of the vendor of feather-dusters, dried melon-seeds, nuts, leeks, fish, fruit, doughnuts, or buns has descended, as traditional, through the centuries. The native of Como could then buy of the stout cook, in cap and apron, at the corner, presiding over furnace and marmite of hot bubbling oil, a dainty morsel, crisp and tempting, equivalent to the slice of *polenta*, little fish, or bit of artichoke of his descendants. The cook is as old as Pompeii, thus depicted, at least. The vendor of hot sausages, a delicacy imported from Gaul, smoked, was also there to serve a portion from a covered dish. A goblet of honey wine was refreshing, on occasion, as were the *crustularii*, slices of toasted bread, eggs, and pastry. The illumination of the town must have been inadequate before the fourth century, as even Rome lacked sufficient light, except on the celebration of such fêtes as the honours paid to Cæsar after quelling the Catiline conspiracy.

Thus little Como acquired the dimensions of a

A World's Shrine

town of importance while apparently insignificant. A tiny queen of a tiny realm, the city ruled all those villages situated on the border of the lake. At times these were mutinous, treacherous, and disloyal. Now Domaso required to be punished and pardoned, with the exaction of tribute, and the rule of Como was pushed to the Valtellina and Coire. Now little Gravedona, Menaggio, or Bellaggio plotted darkly with such foes as Milan, in the strife of Guelph and Ghibelline factions, when Como was but a shuttlecock tossed between rival German emperor and French king. The history of Como, in miniature, is that of Italy. The doughty capital maintained a footing under diverse patron princes, and defied neighbours, as well as essayed to strengthen its borders against foreign foes. Plutarch mentioned Milan as a populous city. Como came, in due course of years, to enjoy more secure roads, free of robbers (*Masnadieri*), dug trenches, and added buttresses to the walls.

Across the centuries, behold the Cavalier Arnaldo Caligno meeting Gilardo of Nonza in

Across the Centuries

single combat for the glory of their respective towns in 1120. The struggle between Como and Milan of 1127 was still more momentous than individual rivalry. Milan was aided by Pavia, Novara, Asti, Vercelli, Cremona, Piacenza, Parma, Mantua, Ferrara, and Bologna. These allies brought four towers of wood, covered with leather, and four engines to shoot stone missiles for the siege. In vain Como covered her fortifications with hides, flexible boughs, and boats, the women and boys assisting in the work. The place was forced to capitulate on August twenty-seventh to so many foes, and the inhabitants abandoned their post during the night, and fled to various asylums. Native poets compare the disaster to the fall of Troy. Milan boasted that Como was rased, and the ground sown with salt in complete desolation, but the statement is false, as many ancient buildings, relics of the Roman occupation remained after the disaster. The Villa Fossani of Paolo Giovio, the reputed site of Pliny's birthplace, in the environs, had still massive fragments, carved marble, and dis-

A World's Shrine

lodged columns, of an earlier structure in recent days. Frederick Barbarossa entered Italy by the route of Trent in 1154. He compelled Milan to free Como of her yoke. In an edict of 1159, he commended Como, and the town remained faithful to him. Praise of this despot emanated from such sources of gratitude, while to the Lombard League he was a monster of cruelty. When Barbarossa lacked silver and had money made of leather, as a substitute, Como must have loyally spent the new currency. The walls rose once more by his order, constructed in a rectangular parallelogram from the Porta Sala to the lake, by Loterio Rusca, captain of the people, with a moat and rampart, planted with trees, of which traces are discernible. Later, a Spanish governor built three towers, and a fortification with eight gates on the side of Milan. Francesco Cigalio wished to rebuild the suburbs of San Rocco and San Bartolomeo at his own expense. The houses were rude, covered with reeds, maize-stalks, straw, or thin shingles, as were those of Alessandria, Milan, and Nice.

Across the Centuries

In the year 1209, the municipality ordered the use of tiles. The three castles erected to defend the town were the *Nuovo*, above San Martino, Ceruasino, and Baradello. Quarters were apportioned to the garrison, and there was a Palace of the Podesta. Valiant Como again prepared to hold head with enemies, and set up her own *carroccio*, the car invented by the warrior Bishop of Milan, Ariberto, to assemble the citizens to arms. The vehicle had four painted wheels, a mast in the centre, surmounted by a golden apple, from which floated the standard of the Commune, together with the cross, or some symbol of the town. Two pairs of oxen, decked with coloured trappings, and preceded by trumpeters, dragged this car, which was the rallying-point even in such engagements as the famous battle of Legnano, when the power of Barbarossa was finally overthrown by the League of the Lombard cities. Como lost a great protector, yet was swayed by all the events of the date, the struggle of personal egotism in magistrates and governors, or the wider impulse of

A World's Shrine

romance and adventure aroused by the Crusades, and the marvellous tales of the riches of the Orient. In 1288, the plague laid a cold hand on all this world, yet did not wholly check the vital development in the soul of man of life and beauty amidst such surroundings of nature. In 1403, Como was sacked by Pandolfo Malatesta, who stormed the place by the round tower. The love of power and luxury grew apace in all these communities. Gian Galeazzo Visconti began to build the Milan Cathedral with the aid of German architects. Como, in her day, erected her Duomo and Broletto, side by side, with knotted shaft, many-coloured marbles, red, white, and dark-grey, arcaded corbels, and doorways of the Lombard character of the late Gothic, with hint of the presence of Bramante and Giotto in the task. Gian Galeazzo gave a banquet when the Bishop of Novara, Pietro di Candia, had delivered an oration on the Piazza of San Ambrogio, at Milan. The vessels were of precious metals at this sumptuous entertainment, with draperies of silk. The guests were refreshed with distilled waters

THE CATHEDRAL OF COMO

for the hands, and given marchpane, and cakes of pine-nuts, gilded, bearing the arms stamped on them of His Serene Highness, and served with cups of white wine. This was truly a golden feast, fulfilling the curious idea that food silvered or gilded signified delicious luxury. Hare, pheasants, turkeys, mutton, sausage with Greek wine, and fowls served to garnish two whole bears, gilded, with citron, two kids, a silver shell containing an entire stag gilded, a tortoise silvered, and platters of trout, lampreys, and sturgeon. Four peacocks in their plumage, galantines, pastry, fresh almonds, peaches, syrups, and Malvasia flanked these triumphs of the culinary art of the time.

Como, also exercised hospitality at this date. The record is given of a citizen who spread a banquet with three calves, fifteen kids, one hundred pigeons and quails, ten hares, twelve rabbits, and forty pheasants, with pastry, tarts, ragouts with sugar, and three casks of wine.

The folly of feminine attire was freely satirised in the descendants of Pliny's mother and wife at Como, under the rule of Francesco Sforza, as

A World's Shrine

indeed, the earlier, classical ladies had been ridiculed by Martial and Juvenal. The women were taxed with finding themselves embellished by voluminous dresses, with trains from the collar, large sleeves, rich cloaks and muffs, the chemise embroidered with gold, ten *braccia* of the linen of Rheims not being more than sufficient for a garment, until they resembled a cask. The hair was short, like that of a man, and shaved on the temples, as the head was covered with a net of coloured silk, ribbons, pins, plumes, and flowers. The robe was cloth-of-gold, with velvet girdle and pocket, the bosom uncovered, and many gems worn.

Across the centuries the first printing-press reached the shores of Como, invented by John Gutenberg of Mayence, the roll of papyrus having yielded place to sheepskin, and the twelfth century triumphed with paper made of rags. If the two Plinys quitted their niche beside the portal of the Como Cathedral to inspect the printing-press what must have been the emotions — even as bloodless shades — of these note-taking citizens?

Across the Centuries

Charles V. visited Como in 1541 with enduring result in Spanish rule.

The French Revolution struck this tiny paradise like a tidal wave in 1796. Equality and liberty electrified the atmosphere of the lake border with the donning of red caps. La Carmagnole was sung by all ranks. The town was re-baptised. The Piazza del Duomo became della Libertà; the Contrada Odelscalchi della Temperanza; Natta, veneration for the laws; Giovio, hatred of tyranny; and San Giacomo, brotherhood. When Bonaparte came he was welcomed as the Caporaletto, and shared the public enthusiasm. Russian and Austrian influences have succeeded. The Latin colony has become a modern town with paved streets, gutters, street-lamps, Persian shutters, and crystal window-panes. The sound of her silk mills is audible through the long hours of the summer day, and a thread may be chosen from the tangled skein of her varied history by the loiterer or the studious which will form a link with all her surroundings as well.

III

THE COUNTRY GENTLEMAN

PLINY the Younger is ever the host who welcomes the visitor to the shores of Como. He is portrayed, with all the skill of the Renaissance, on one side of the portal of the Cathedral, while his worthy uncle, Pliny the Elder, flanks the other. Christianity has unhesitatingly adopted these pagans. If they walked the streets of Como now they would doubtless inspire in their fellow-citizens the same respect for manifold virtues that fell to their portion with their contemporaries.

On a summer day we naturally relegate the senior to the shades, with a passing conviction of the guilty frivolity of our own age in comparison with his edifying example, in favour of the charming personality of the nephew. Every one is familiar with the awe-inspiring zeal in study of

The Country Gentleman

Pliny the Elder. The use of time with him was fate, as with Marlowe. He made notes, or had a slave at his elbow on a journey jotting down memoranda. He served in Germany, returned to Rome, and spoke in the Forum. He was appointed procurator in Spain by Nero, and recalled by Vespasian to command the naval armament at Misenium. He left his nephew one hundred and eighty books in fine writing; thirty six volumes of Natural History; twenty on the subject of the Roman wars in Germany; and thirty-one on the history of his own times. His style lacked the elegance of the Golden Age, we are told. He discussed the stars, the elements, geography, man, animals, plants, and minerals. Buffon said: " Pliny worked on a large canvas, and perhaps too vast: he wished to embrace all: he seemed to have measured nature and found it too small for the capacities of his mind. His Natural History comprises sky and earth, medicine, commerce, navigation, mechanics, the origin of customs; in fact, all human science and arts."

Pliny the Younger must have sadly needed

A World's Shrine

spectacles by the time he had perused his inheritance, if he ever conscientiously read those tomes. To the Plinys is attributed holding a heavy globe of glass, filled with water, to the eye to render objects larger and more distinct. Roger Bacon and Salvino degli Armati, of Florence, were as yet unborn. Also may one venture to infer that there was an element of consolation and relief when the fumes of Vesuvius stifled and extinguished the learned gentleman before he consigned more of his lucubrations to waxen tablet, or papyrus roll? There existed no printing-press and typewriter to keep the world going in his day.

Thus C. Plinius, son of a sister and Lucio Cecilio, a very ancient and noble family of Greek origin, belonging to the Diumvirus of the colony Julia Equestria, stepped on the stage at the age of eighteen years, with the death of his uncle. Let us cling to our idols while we may. The arrow of modern sarcasm has been launched at this paragon. He is pronounced a muff, a tiresome and pedantic prig. French wit terms him "that ninny of a Pliny the Younger, who

The Country Gentleman

studied a Greek oration while Vesuvius engulfed five towns." From our point of view, and especially on the shores of Como, despite flippant aspersions, he shines in the mild radiance of one of the most interesting figures of antiquity. He was born at Como, A. D. 62, in the paternal mansion, situated in a suburb of the town, and approached by a long avenue of trees. Fain would we rebuild that home of the patrician Roman family which was his cradle, out of the fragments of marble columns, cornices, and slabs bearing inscriptions still found near the Lake Larius. Each new-comer may ponder on the matter in his own fashion, and behold rise before his eyes once more the *ostium*, the vestibule, which gave an entrance to the house, the external posts for the support of lamps, the door, not hung on hinges, but with wedge-shaped pins in the hollows above and below, or moved by means of bronze or iron rings, a portal not fastened during the day, and read the *salve*, traced in mosaic, on the threshold. Each can penetrate the inner circle of Roman life by the *atrium*, equivalent to the

A World's Shrine

common hall of the Middle Ages, where the family gathered, from birth to death, with the domestic hearth alight, and the Penates were treasured in little cupboards until relegated by fashion to more distant quarters. The deceased was laid out in state in the *atrium*, and the *imagines*, the waxen masks of forefathers, were suspended on the walls. The mistress of the house was here guardian of the father's strong-box, the household bed, and received all visitors and clients, while her female slaves worked at looms. When the hearth was removed, an altar, or chapel, was accorded the Lares, as the Madonna has now a shrine near the fire of rustic homes in Italy.

Plus ça change, plus c'est la même chose.

Beyond were the *impluvium*, the cistern, or fountain, with four-cornered basins of the inner court, the *cubicula, trinclinia, balinium*, sleeping apartments, and slave quarters. Such was the fabric of Roman family dignity in organisation. Due reverence was paid to the ties of kindred, and kindness manifested to distant relatives.

A gracious vision is vouchsafed to imagination

The Country Gentleman

of Pliny's mother, as a bride, attired in a white tunic, with a yellow veil, and her hair bound up in a net of the same hue, quitting the paternal roof after appropriate ceremonies, whether of the rites of *manus* or *confarreatio*, and escorted in the evening, under the protection of Juno Domiduca, to her new sphere by a procession. Servants carried the basket (*cumerus*) containing the spinning apparatus of the bride, while the Roman *thalassio* replaced, in song, the Greek Hymenæus. Then was the maiden carried over the threshold for good luck, and the door-posts were decorated for the occasion. Madame Plinia must have been one of those matrons above reproach, whose epitaphs record their virtues on the Appian Way, the Portias, the two Arrias, mother and daughter, who formed the solid foundations of State, while the Julias, Messalinas, and Faustinas are much more likely to be selected for portraiture. If the Greek woman was kept shut up in the *gynœkonitis*, the Roman was treated with open regard, as the housewife, mistress of the domestic economy, and instructress of the children.

A World's Shrine

Pliny saw the light of day on the shores of Lake Como. The rights of paterfamilias were those of life and death over the child. Did Madame Plinia, entered upon all the dignity of superintending the household, nourish her son at her own breast, after the example of Cato's mother, and the earlier custom of Greek and Roman women? Rather must we infer that he had a foster parent in one of those sun-bronzed, vigorous peasants, whose descendants deck their heads with silver pins, and ribbons, for he apportioned property in his will to the value of one hundred thousand sesterces to his nurse. A link of warm human interest between the remote past and the present exists in the bequest of Pliny the Younger. The faithful old nurse of all lands is revealed, devoted to the care of master and family. Pliny's registry of birth must have included the depositing of a piece of money at the *ærarium* of the temple of Juno Lucina. He wore the *bulla aurea*, the flat gold amulet, or locket, of children of rank. Assuredly that ancient christening party took place in the Como house when he was nine days old of the *lustratium*, under the divinity Nundina. He was thus admitted to the family circle, while a formal notice of his tender existence was given to the prefect of the Treasury, with the entry in the *Acta diurna*. He received gifts from his parents, relatives, and even the slaves, of the little, metal toys suspended around his neck. He was fed on *puls*, or gruel, until able to partake of the *clusina*, the Etruscan soup of meat and vegetables which became modified into the *minestra* of the land. The slaves and countrywomen did the baking. The Roman boy is said to have had a sort of pastry made for his especial delectation, which no doubt would be appreciated by the juvenile palate still.

Thus did Pliny attain the dignity of sharing the domestic meals, the matitudinal *jantaculum* of bread, seasoned with salt, cheese, olives, dried grapes, eggs, or *mulsum ;* the noon *prandium* of warm and cold dishes; and the *cena*, supper, the most important repast of the day.

Pliny is not to be relegated to the ranks of

schoolboy. Schools existed at an early date. The first mention of them is reputed to have been the young girl Virginia tripping along the streets of Rome, and espied by the evil Appius Claudius. How readily the familiar image of the dilatory urchin loitering towards the goal is conjured from the shadows of the past in the mention of Horace brought to Rome by his father, as the school at Venusium was inferior, or Ovid fetched from Sulino to the capital by his brother, for the same reason. Oh, there were satchels, rulers, counting-tables, desks, and pockets in which to hoard treasures in those days! The school was held at a very early hour of the morning. The holidays occurred at the season of the vintage and the olive harvest. Our young gentleman, who is considered the most nearly in touch with modern life of any Roman, had no such public education. After the conquest of southern Italy, the Romans were brought in contact with the Greeks, and had domestic *pedagogi* in order that the children might early learn to speak Greek, much as the foreign governess instructs infantile lispings of French, German, or English. Prudent fathers inclined to private instruction. The elder Cato gave lessons to his son, although he had a Greek grammarian as tutor. There being no royal road to learning, Pliny was doubtless first trained by the slave *litterator* in reading, writing, and arithmetic, imparted in two ways, by signs with the fingers, or a counting-table and stones, the *abacus* and *calculi*, those equivalents of slates and blackboards. Geography, mythology, and critical readings of Homer, Terence, Virgil, and Horace with the grammarian followed, with the ultimate aim of gaining distinction in the lecture room, and rhetoric. Nor were games and martial exercises forgotten, although he is described as of a fragile constitution. The long robe of childhood was exchanged for the *toga virilis*, the citizen's dress, at the age of fourteen or sixteen, with the deposit of money in the temple of Juventas. Public speaking, the much prized forensic eloquence, was next studied. He had for preceptor the wise and polished Quintilian. He also cherished

A World's Shrine

much esteem for another instructor in the philosopher Eucrates, found by Pliny in the depths of Syria, where he was serving as a soldier. Eucrates, a disciple of Plato, subtle in dispute, making a war on vice, inspired in discourse, reconciled Pliny to philosophy, and the just discernment of pleasure and duty. Pliny recalled the lessons of this sage of austere visage and long hair and beard all his life.

The youth departed from his home in the suburb of Como to enter the world. His tutor, Aristones, had been zealous and prudent. Instructed in oratory, Pliny entered the arena modestly in a criminal case, as was the custom. Eloquence is composed of three elements, according to Quintilian, — to read, write, and speak well. Thus Pliny declaimed in public, wrote dialogues, poems, and pages of history. As a young man he composed little verses of society, in the fashion of the time, as a recreation from serious labours. Spurrina was to him an edifying example of well-regulated age, rising early to the routine of a day of gentle exercise, study, the bath, playing a game of tennis, and fed at a frugal board spread with massive silver utensils, and the brass of Corinth. When Pliny appeared on the public piazza, in a white robe, may he not have saluted the lowest plebeian, soliciting his vote for office, and often buying it with money? The politeness of the Prætor, Mancinus, in explaining to the people in the Forum some pictures exhibited, for which they made him consul the next year, would have been a natural trait of amiability in Pliny the Younger. He seems to have been sent to Athens for further culture. His lines were cast in pleasant places throughout his career. He did not need to complain, with Martial, of being invited to sup with the rich Mancinus, when a sucking pig was divided among sixty hungry guests, while the host ate grapes, apples as sweet as honey, pomegranates of Carthage, and olives of Picenum.

In public life the place in history of Pliny is at the base of the column of Trajan. Both gain by such propinquity, and their memory has been cherished by succeeding centuries; so long do the good deeds of men live after them. Trajan, born in Spain, has been considered the first provincial to gain the rank of emperor. He was less exclusively Roman than his predecessors. He built monuments of his own greatness in all parts of the known universe. An arch of Trajan stands at Benevento, and another at Ancona. He constructed a bridge of twenty arches on the Rhine, and a rampart above the Danube. He aspired to becoming a ruler not only of the Romans, but of the entire human race. In his military career he defeated Decebalus, and made Dacia a Roman province, took Ctesiphon, the capital of Parthia, and descended the Tigris to the Persian Gulf. One of the greatest and best of emperors, he is praised for his moderation, simplicity of living, and excellent judgment. He presided at the tribunal which condemned Saint Ignatius. Ampère compares Trajan to Washington, as a Roman general instead of a Virginia planter, yet both inspired by the same sentiment of duty in defending the frontiers of country against an enemy. Trajan, with his firm

The Country Gentleman

mien, would have marched as far as India, if necessary, and Washington, the friend of peace, threatened by England during his presidency, prepared to hold head modestly with the foe.

Pliny practised law at Rome, held public offices, and became Proconsul of Bithynia in 103. He wrote the famous letter to Trajan in which he bore testimony to the morality of the Christians. Pliny consulted the emperor in all matters of difficulty, and even of the small interests of towns in Asia. The replies of Trajan were models of good sense and brevity, gravity, and the conciseness known as *imperatoria brevitas*, whether a decision on the building of a new bath by the inhabitants of Prusium, or giving the citizens of Amasia permission to cover a stagnant stream. What was the actual opinion of tolerant master and minister of the sect of Christians? Pliny does not seem to have been especially interested in their tenets, although he was humane in disposition towards an inoffensive body. Trajan, with his principles of Roman distrust of individual liberty, independent associations, civil

A World's Shrine

or religious, and the aim of centralising all government, still manifested true clemency to the followers of Christ, and a wish to avoid persecuting them. The Middle Ages accorded his memory fresh fame. Pope Gregory the Great considered that the soul of such a good heathen emperor should be saved by the intercession of religion. Trajan was prayed for in Purgatory and redeemed. The doctors of divinity combated such remission of the damnation of a soul, but the saints have accepted the deliverance of Trajan. The Greek church has this phrase in its ritual: "O God, pardon him as Thou hast pardoned Trajan by St. Gregory." Thomas Aquinas, as the Angelical Doctor, has sought to explain how, without heresy, this charitable miracle was accomplished. Dante places Trajan in Paradise. During a long and glorious reign the devotion of the people caused his portrait busts and statues, common-place, with a low forehead, and even lacking heroic or benevolent expression, to be multiplied. At his death these memorials were not destroyed. " More happy than Augustus or better than Trajan" became a flattering formula of address to powerful sovereigns. Even more majestic is the suggestion that in Wallachia and other Danubian provinces, where this mighty ruler planted the Roman eagle, previously cast down under Domitian, the souvenir of him has lingered with a mythological significance. The thunder is the voice of Trajan, and the Milky Way his high-road in the skies. Legend is here conquest and apotheosis. In the twelfth century the municipality of Rome took measures to protect the edifices erected by Pliny's master, because of the virtues of an emperor who merited immortality.

Mellow sunshine of all the passing years traces the marvellous story unrolled on Trajan's column in the Eternal City. This monument, once crowned by his statue, holding a gilded ball, comprises his history, pedestal of his power, trophy of his glory, and guardian of his ashes. The bas-reliefs are the recital of an ancient *volumen*, the memoirs, carved in stone, of his campaigns, more enduring than the writings of Marius Maximius, Fabius Marcellinus, Aurelius Verus, Statius Valens, or the Greek poems of Caninius Rufus. The homage of a conquered world may be traced, mounting the shaft to the feet of the emperor, Roman soldiers crossing rivers, Dacian ambassadors presenting tribute, the building of camps, and the siege of towns.

Pliny's place was at the base of the column, writing the panegyric of his patron, who sought to occupy himself with the well-being of all classes in his vast domain. The praises of Pliny were couched in the most flowery language, and extol Trajan for affording a spectacle "not destined to soften the soul, but calculated to stimulate courage, to familiarise with noble wounds, and to inspire us with scorn of death." He was in himself rather a conscientious minister than one born to govern.

Pliny enters on the most interesting phase of his career to posterity when he returned from foreign service, and became the country gentleman. He liked to escape from town life to the rural home, in common with his contemporaries, and mankind in general. He enjoyed a suburban retreat in a pavilion at Tusculum, another on the Tiber, and a property facing the Tyrrhenian Sea, the Laurentine villa described by him, with the air as pure as that of Attica, amidst the thyme of Hymettus, terraces, galleries, and circular chambers, screened from the north by gardens and pine-woods. He sought his native Como, where he had several mansions. The site of the charming spot called Comedy, situated on the brink of the water, and of another abode on a height known as Tragedy, have become traditional.

Behold our amiable host, "*le plus doux des hommes*," quitting his house on the Esquiline to linger in the pure air of the Apennines, or push on to Como. No direct train of the day or night express swept him over plain and through tunnelled hillside. He departed from Rome by one of her four roads which traversed the land like arteries, probably the great northern route, the Flaminian Way, which led from Porta Salara by Soracte and the Sabine hills, northeast to An-

A World's Shrine

cona, Rimini, thence known as Via Emilia, to Piacenza, Milan, and Cisalpine Gaul. "All roads lead to Rome."

Pliny does not seem to have built roads, like the Censor, C. Flaminius, but availed himself of Roman munificence, public and private. The Curator often spent large sums out of private fortunes on repairs. Slaves and convicts laboured to drain off the rain, and trace the route with reference to the nature of the rocky *statumen*, a lower bed of rough stones being omitted if the rock itself could be carefully levelled to receive *rudus* and *neucleus*, on which the lava pavement was bedded. In marshy districts the *statumen* was replaced by wooden piles, and frequently in valleys a viaduct of masonry was substituted. Ditches (*fossæ*) were dug on either side, and milestones, *milliaria*, erected. Special rates for repairs were paid. In Rome each house was taxed for the pavement opposite. Julius Cæsar was Curator of the Via Appia, and Cornutius Tertullus of Via Emilia. *Ramuli* were small cross-roads leading from main thoroughfares,

The Country Gentleman

and the *vide vicinales* were sustained as parish dues under local officers, *magistri pagorum*. The Flaminian coin of Augustus represents him crowned by Victory, in a *biga* drawn by elephants, and on the reverse the Via Flaminia carried on arches.

Oh, that much vaunted civilisation would more frequently imitate the Roman, and build roads for fellow-man out of a portion of the wealth lavished on charities, college libraries, and municipal art museums! Consider the satisfaction of giving a bridge to a whole countryside. Even in a spiritualised sense it were better to remove the stone from the path, like the old men and women of certain Oriental countries, for those who come after, than to place more obstructions of jealousy and envy in the way.

Pliny must have discarded his *toga* for the *pœnula*, and assumed travelling-shoes, then set forth in the *lectica*, litter, through crowded streets, exchanged for horses, mules, or convenient vehicles of the cabriolet sort, with leather hood and curtains, accompanied by Numidian

A World's Shrine

outriders, while the attendants followed in the *petorrita*. Such journeying brought him to the brink of the crystal cup of Lake, where he is still the pervading presence. He was admirable in all walks of life, a just patron, a senator, an avocat, cherishing a love of glory and renown, and holding to all those ancient institutions which endeared him to Trajan. Returning to Como he established schools, with a stipend of thirty thousand sesterces annually for the benefit of the town. He further endowed orphans of impoverished families. Pliny as the letter-writer is still quoted. He left ten volumes of correspondence esteemed the most precious epistolary relics of Roman life, after those of Cicero. A telegraphic century may well pause in a summer hour on Como, and reflect on the letter-writing of past generations. Will the art soon be lost? Pliny is an august and distant shade, as ancestor, with Cicero, of all that graceful and sprightly company, the Italians who cultivated the gift in Latin, such as Galileo and Bentivoglio, Saint-Evremond, Voltaire, or Madame de Sévigné, in happiest inspiration,

The Country Gentleman

Pope, Gray, Cowper, and Byron. In Roman literature, descriptive, biographical, and in anecdote men wrote their own lives. Pliny's correspondence is a full portraiture of the Roman gentleman, whether with Silius Italicus, the wealthy versifier, Passienus Paulus, Caninius Rufus, Pomponius Saturninus, or other friends. His epistles were polished with the care of a fine writer, who combines grace and lightness with seriousness. His dissertation on style in the twentieth letter might be modern:

"Certainly conciseness is not to be neglected when language permits; but I also maintain that it is often treason not to say all possible, to half trace that which should be stamped on souls. Do not scorn the resources of words; they add to the force and lustre of thought. Our passion penetrates the nature of our audience as iron enters a solid body: a single blow is insufficient, it must be redoubled. To Lysias, the king of conciseness, to the old Cato, who would have blushed to utter a superfluous word, I oppose the abundance of Eschinus, of Demosthenes, of Cicero. Cicero said that in his opinion the finest harangue was the longest."

A World's Shrine

This excellent Pliny, benevolent, peaceable, polite to all, honest, and actuated by a tolerant wisdom of demeanour to his fellow-creatures, wrote on all topics of the day. Now fancy led him to describe the emotions of a sentimental dolphin on the coast of Africa, and again he invented a ghost story of a haunted house at Athens. One element of his correspondence concerned the rights of pillaged provinces, or the repairs of the Emilian road. He lamented the death, at the age of fourteen years, of the amiable daughter of Fundanius. He gave items of life in the capital, weddings, betrothals, a testament to sign, the son of a friend assuming the virile robe. He invited Clarus to supper, promising the guest a salad, three snails, a cake, two eggs, wine mingled with snow, olives of Andalusia, gourds, and shalots, while a comedian, or a flute-player should enliven the dessert. But Clarus failed to appear. The feast spread by Pythagoras was more to his taste than eggs, lettuce, snails, and shalots. Fie, then! He sought a richer mansion, more succulent temptations, the finest oysters of

The Country Gentleman

the Lucrine Lake, exquisite viands, and wines perfumed with a hundred leaves, with Spanish dancers as fresh and young as a garland of roses, to charm the revellers. In married life Pliny's wife, the lady Calphurnia, a sympathetic companion of mind and heart, often held one of his works in her hand, a circumstance on which he dwelt with much complacency. The dutiful spouse listened behind a curtain when he read in public. Pliny wept for the death of faithful slaves, rejoicing that many had first received their freedom. He wore mourning for his friends.

Como was the shrine of his heart. He was born there, and, become rich and powerful, he wished to live on the borders of Larius. He was familiar with the trees, the cedars, the beech, the alders, myrtles, and laurels. He wrote to Catinius: "Are you fond of study, fishing, or hunting? You can enjoy all these occupations in our mansion on the Lake of Como. The lake furnishes the fish, the woods yield stags and deer, while the admirable tranquillity of this delightful retreat

A World's Shrine

invites the mind to study, and the calm leisure for which I sigh as a sick person for fresh wine, the tepid bath, or healing waters."

Pliny the Youngest, in the twentieth century tenants his villa on Como. He is a cosmopolitan of good family, gently reared, and carefully educated. Possibly, like his earlier prototype, he resembles Monsieur Banal; being routine fused with egotism, mediocre, with no rash enthusiasm to disarrange the order of things. Is there anything new under the sun? Pliny the Younger lamented the degeneracy of the times thus: "Senators and judges come to be chosen for their income, and magistrates and generals regard money as their chief title to distinction. . . . All the noble pursuits of life and liberal arts have fallen to the ground, and servitude alone is profitable. In various ways all men care for money, and for money alone."

Would it be possible for the modern gentleman of birth and fortune to weigh the political phases of his day in a more pessimistic spirit?

The suburban residence, dedicated to a lux-

The Country Gentleman

urious sojourn of a few months, is completely appointed in a sumptuous manner, according to the requirements of the master. The earlier Pliny might have smiled at the ménage, since royal palaces are scarcely furnished with the staff of menials essential to his comfort in the slaves of town and country houses. Pliny the Youngest may have his confidential and discreet man servant, butler, *chef*, with attendant myrmidons and maids. The other Pliny had natives of Asia, Syrians, Lydians, Carians, Mysians, Italians, Cappadocians, Celts, or Germans skilled in agriculture in his retinue, in lieu of deft footmen, grooms, gardeners, or valets. A sandal boy, (*calceator*) put on the master's shoes, and ran errands, page fashion; the *vestiplicus* was a folder of clothes; librarians, scribes, readers, domestic nurses, and doctors, a small army of dusters and sweepers appertained to the household. A *Corinthus* cared for the Corinthian vases, while the superintendent *villicus*, bailiff, directed gamekeepers, vine-dressers, sowers, reapers, and tenders of horses, mules, oxen, and sheep.

A World's Shrine

Probably in all the guile of the servants' hall the average domestic is not more subtly versed than was the slave of antiquity. These were taught to carve, as an accomplishment, to the sound of music, to cool apartments with fans, move about among guests, girt with napkins and towels, with bowls of water for finger dipping, carry wine-cups crowned with flowers, and serve the meats of those banquets where the shield of Minerva was heaped with fish, game, and fruits. In matters gastronomical, even if deeply versed in all the shades of culinary science, the Pliny of our time could scarcely teach that Roman gentleman much. Doubtless the classical cook was skilled in imitating the flavours of rare fish in coarse ones, as well as the artist of the kitchen of Louis XIV., or to impart a semblance of fowls and game on fast days to the *maigre* of vegetables. The profound system of preparing a meal for the hunger of youth, for maturity when appetite comes in eating, and a surprise at the end of a repast for jaded palates may be very old. The sweet of milk and sugar, the saltness of the marine wave,

The Country Gentleman

the acid of citron, the bitter of chicory, the sharpness of spices, and the astringency of pomegranates, as aiding these results, were understood at a date when Vitellius sent to Syria for the pistachio nut to add to his condiments of oil, vinegar, aromatic plants, mint, saffron, or aniseed.

Is the youngest epicure a connoisseur of wine, fish, fruit? Pliny the Younger tasted thirty varieties of pears, of which the best were the Crustumian, the Falernian, Syrian, and the *volema*, the first pear in size. Plums of Damascus and Armeniaca, cherries, quinces, figs, medlars, mulberries, almonds, and chestnuts fell to his portion. He must have been a *gourmet* in fish, from the gustatus (whet) of salted slices, served with eggs, rue, and cybium, the sauce-piquante of anchovy, the garum, the edible purple mussel, to the mullet, the little gobius of Venice, the rhombus (turbot) of Ravenna, the sea-eel (*murdena*) of Sicily and Tartessus, haddock, conger, and lupus, sea-wolf. He was an authority on wine, whether pure Falernian or the beverages mingled with perfumed oils, aloes and myrrh.

Pliny the Youngest is usually contented with his bath-room, if a tiny chamber, vaulted, tesselated with marble, furnished with *douche*, and a coffin-shaped tub, like the little temple of a nymph in the Pitti Palace at Florence, with delightfully refreshing toilet waters and soaps, fresh linen, brushes and sponges additional.

The bath signified to Pliny the Younger the *frigidarium*, either public or private, the swimming-tanks of the *natatorium*, the *caldarium*, painted ceilings, mosaic pavements, columns, bronze seats, glass utensils, wash-balls, fragrant oils of crocus and saffron, pomades, the *nardinium* made of the blossoms of the nard grass of Arabia and India, and the odoriferous powders, *diapasmata* of the Greek gymnasium, and *thermæ*. Hygienic exercises were not neglected in those earlier times. Old and young played ball, the *follis* ('big'), and the *pila* (small), running and leaping in games, the indolent and decrepit riding on horseback, or being borne out in litters.

The Country Gentleman

Our patricians have been wont to attire themselves in soft raiment. Pliny the Younger wore garments of wool (*lanea*), silk (*serica*), linen and cotton (*bombycina*). Pliny the Youngest may smile superciliously as he contemplates his neat gaiters, walking, golf, and tennis shoes in comparison with the foot-gear of his predecessor, the sandals, attached with thongs to instep and ankle. Likewise it must be confessed that the ideas of Pliny the Younger as to time-keeping, the sun-dial as an obelisk, or a hollow hemisphere, with the hours divided by eleven lines, and cloudy weather marked by such early hour-glasses as water-clocks, the clepsydra did not equal the system of noting the fleeting moments of his successor, from the musical chime of clocks, French, Swiss, and of Black Forest make, to the stem-winding chronometer of a vest pocket, or Mrs. Pliny's bracelet.

The Como Villa is illuminated by electricity. Pale moons and suns gleam amidst the dusky shrubbery of garden alleys, and flowers of silk and tinted crystal screen the lamps of alcove and

A World's Shrine

corridor. The ancient Roman had the *lucerna*, oil fed, in graceful designs of terra-cotta and bronze, decorated with garlands, masks, dolphins, peacocks, or apes, swung on chains; slips of pine for torches; tallow and wax candles (*sebaceæ*), with wicks of rush, the indigenous papyrus, hemp (*cannabis*), and the leaves of *verbascum;* lanterns framed in metal, glass, or thin plates of horn; candelabra, and the *lampadaria*, the column to hold lamp or torch.

In the value attached to his library the ancient yielded nothing to posterity. Do the shelves of the Como mansion boast the latest editions of Quaritch, the Kelmscott Press, *éditions de luxe* of Paris and Berlin, as a resource of leisure? Pliny the Younger, in his prime, treasured in receptacles of precious wood and metal boxes the rolls wrapped in parchment, dyed purple and yellow, and held by a stick with a gilded knob, the title and index attached, tinted with red *coccum*, while a portrait of the author adorned the front page, and the writing on leather and linen in ink of Chinese pigment, the juice of sepia, and of the flax stalk. Another form of book was the strips of Egyptian papyrus glued together. Eight qualities of paper are mentioned by him, the Augustana, Claudiana, and Liviana as superior, *charta dentata*, with the surface polished by the tooth of some animal to produce a glossy face for the pen, like a " hot pressed " sheet, the *charta bibula*, transparent and spongy, and inferior sorts for wrappings and merchandise. Educated slaves cared for the *volumen*, smoothed with pumice stone the *libellus*, a little book consisting of a few leaves of parchment bound together, or the liber compiled of the rind of the Egyptian papyrus. In addition they transcribed and bound books, were in charge of the master's correspondence, and compiled the index. Inkstands were wrought of silver and bronze, and the reed, *calamus*, the usual pen.

Pliny's picture gallery was arranged with reference to a northern light, in order that the sun might not injure the *tabulæ*, wooden panels inserted in the wall, or hung against it.

He was of a delicate constitution, and may

not the pure air of Como be an attraction to the modern sojourner in a mild climate, as well? The proverb says that every man is his own doctor at the age of forty, or a fool. Distrust of the learned fraternity was early manifested at Rome. The first Greek physician Archagathus, practised in the Eternal City A. D. 535, and inspired doubt of the science altogether. Cato warned his son against the pursuit of medicine, and all doctors. Pliny the Youngest may keep his own pharmacopœia of compressed tabloids or homeopathic phials, and resort to certain Spas in their season, while lacking the robust fibre of a horse-racing, Alpine-climbing, polo, cricket, and foot-ball-playing era.

The latter receives daily, almost hourly, his harvest of letters, post-cards, advertisements, pamphlets, and late editions of journalistic cable news from the four quarters of the globe. He would be dull otherwise, and defrauded of his rights as a citizen of the world.

Lo! Pliny the Younger did not fare badly in these matters on Como. The ancients had no

The Country Gentleman

newspapers, but there was a public dissemination of news on the piazza, in the forum, at the baths, at clubs, by means of the barber, the doctor, and the scribe. As another compensation for the daily journals, copies of the *acta diurna publica*, or *urbana*, were despatched to all parts of the Roman Empire. These acts, or chronicles, were begun in Cæsar's first consulate, or not much earlier. They comprised important events, new laws, annuals, maxims of other times, decrees of the Senate, edicts of the magistrates, fires, sacrifices, the announcement of festivals, processions, births, marriages, divorces, and deaths. The compilations were made by the *actuarii*, appointed under the director of the *tabulæ publicæ*. Bulletins were written down, tables exposed for any one to read and copy. Scribes copied out these *acta* for pay, while others made extracts for subscribers sent to distant provinces.

Does the youngest Pliny dally with the finest French and English stationary in his correspondence? His predecessor was also remembered by the post; only, his letters were written on thin tablets of wood, *tabellæ*, covered with wax, or on parchment, bound together with linen threads, or sealed with a ring, brought by couriers and messengers. Also, his pocket note-book consists of small tablets, with ornamented covers of gold, silver, or ivory, and a *stilus*, pointed at one end, and blunted for erasure at the other.

The youngest Pliny is the finest fruit of civilisation, but he can scarcely follow a more noble model than the ancient Roman gentleman. Consider the delicacy of consideration in his gift to Quintilian of a dowry for his daughter, when the philosopher had lost his son. The mode of bestowing a benefit is as much as the donation.

"No one knows better than I, my venerated master, the moderation of your wishes; I know, also, that your daughter has been reared in all the virtues worthy of the child of Quintilian and the granddaughter of Tutilius; but whom to-day you give to Nonius Celer, a very worthy man, honoured with important duties. Our child should be surrounded by those belongings suited to the rank of her husband; this distinction without augmenting our dignity gives us independent

The Country Gentleman

ease. You are rich in gifts of the soul, and other fortune you have always disdained; suffer therefore, my second father, in the name of the many benefactions you have heaped upon me that I give to your dear daughter fifty thousand sesterces. I count on the modesty of the little present to obtain the permission which I solicit of your indulgence."

Consider the munificence and Christian kindness of his last testament. He did not possess the wealth of a Marcus Crassus, yet he paid the debts of a friend, gave portions to faithful servants, bestowed three hundred thousand sesterces on Romanzio Fermo, the land to the old nurse, and public benefits to Como. He was the friend of Tacitus, and these two upheld the antique creed that honour and probity still remained among men.

Pliny the Younger, beside the portal of the Como cathedral, is ever the host welcoming all comers to this summer Eden.

IV

A VANISHED HOUSE

TWILIGHT on Como is the calm transition hour when the rich colouring of day, flaming in amber, copper, and golden hues on the peaks, has been quenched in soft, pearly-grey tones about the base of cliffs, where a silvery veil already gathers with the mists of night. Stars begin to sparkle in the vault of sky above the lake, and a ray of light trembles here and there on the surface of the water.

The Berlin professor wanders apart, responsive to the spell of the spot. He is a quiet man, large, bearded, and spectacled, affable in manner to all in the casual intercourse of travelling acquaintance, *Reisebekamtschaft*, and fond of talking with the natives of a country in out-of-the-

A Vanished House

way nooks. All day he has walked and botanised with his wife, a buxom dame of the Frau Buchholtz type, and smiling daughters. Now he enters the boat of Memory, and steers his way on the unruffled lake to a shrine of fancy. Already the fishermen have prepared their nets in the depths, guarded by an empty boat, with a bell adjusted to ring with every motion caused by a passing ripple. The bell guides his course. That fitful cadence, the merest tinkle of a prosaic warning to respect the rights of a humble neighbour, is symbolical to the savant, calling to him from the immeasurable distance of the Past.

Pliny the Younger built his Villa of Comedy on the brink of the tide. Tradition places the site at Euripus, the lower portion of the Tremezzino, beyond the promontory of Balbinello, or Lavedo, where wall and column have settled beneath the current. The vague outline of possibility in skirting curves of the shore only enhances the charm of endless speculation as to the actual site of the famous residence. All the witchery appertaining to submerged towns, and

A World's Shrine

church towers that still chime their own knell in ghostly fashion, whether of sea-coast, or inland rivers, belongs to Pliny's vanished home. When the level of the Lake Celano, the ancient Fucinus, was unusually low, in 1752, a city was uncovered, and the statues of Claudius and Agrippina revealed. Thus may Pliny's Villa rise once more as perfect as the fabric of a vision.

The Berlin professor is not solitary in the craft of memory. A spectral crew of kindred souls have already boarded his skiff in sympathetic unison. Salmasius, Casaubon, Lipsius, and Becker share his reveries in this branch of archæology, the study of antiquities.

"Take my glass of intuitive intelligence and spy at the boundaries of Pliny's mansion," quoth Becker.

"Strive to live over again Pliny's daily life here," echoes Lipsius.

"Yes; decide for yourself, if this delicious retreat served Pliny to attain the felicity of well-being of Horace in realising all his dreams: honourable leisure, a modest fortune equal to

A Vanished House

his desires, and a corner of the earth between the shadow and the silence," muses Salmasius.

The Berlin professor needs no second bidding. In the twilight the sheet of water all about his bark is a magic mirror. He longs to plunge beneath that crystal barrier, and roam through the precincts of Pliny's Villa of Comedy, described by the owner as having a court shaded by plane trees, a gallery flanking spaces of green turf, fields stretching in the rear, apple trees, shaded alleys, and arbours of acanthus, trellised and supported on columns. The interior offered a cool retreat for sultry hours. The walls were painted to represent birds, flowers, and foliage, as at Pompeii and Herculaneum. A cabinet of study was finished in marble, while statues and pictures adorned the other apartments. Pliny reclined in his gardens, and listened to the melody of flowing waters. He could cast a line into the wave, and fish, since the finest eels swam up to the very door. His note-book was ever open to jot down his thoughts, possibly in the short-hand method which he states came into use under Cæsar's rule. Also

A World's Shrine

he gave his opinions more ample scope in dictation to Notarius, the slave at his elbow. His letter to Tacitus, descriptive of boar-hunting, has been praised for grace:

"The snares were set, and with my tablets in my hand, I awaited the game in order not to return to the house empty. All succeeded with me; I filled my tablets, and behold me sure that Minerva, as well as Diana, is pleased with our hills. Try this sport: it is admirable. How much exhilaration is excited by the hunt. At the same time how the calm of the forests, the silence of the woods, and solitude are favourable to meditation."

His invitation to Rufus is no less charming:

"Leave mean and sordid cares to others, and devote yourself to study in a profound and rich seclusion. Make this your affair, your leisure, your work and rest, your thought in wakeful hours, and the motive of your dreams."

Doubtless Pliny entertained society here with nice tact. If he had a Catius, who placed the culinary art at the summit of human felicity, for guest, he prepared a kid of the vineyards, the

A Vanished House

Umbrian boar fed on red acorns, mushrooms of the meadows, cray-fish of Misenium, scallops of Tarentum, or the Melian crane. The jaded wine-bibber was tempted with roasted shrimps, African cockles, and the Venusian grape preserved.

Did the host ever nod drowsily in the Villa of Comedy, with the very foundations gently lapped by the tide? Pliny the Elder scorned indulgence in sleep as a sheer waste of time. One must suspect the nephew of taking an occasional siesta, soothed by his own poetical fancies in such a retreat as grottoes shaded by a drapery of fern-like vines and plants, or subterranean chambers hollowed out of the cliffs and rocks, adapted to repose. Even the terrible fever of insomnia of a Mæcenas, lulled in vain by soft music and falling waters, might have yielded to oblivion here.

Verily the ancient Roman studied the means of enjoying refreshing coolness on his country property. He paid dearly for such luxury on occasion. There was rheumatism in those classical days, the "thorn in the flesh" from which Renan believed the Apostle Paul suffered. The

A World's Shrine

Roman seems to have boiled himself in all the hot springs and mud baths of Europe from Aix-la-Chapelle, Spa, Wiesbaden, Teplitz, or Ragatz to Acqui and Ischia.

In the twilight the Berlin professor has a vision of the submerged mansion. He discerns the actual shimmer of Hymettan and Pentelic marbles beneath the ripples; the tawny lustre of the Numidian yellow antique; Carian veins of dull green and brown in dislodged cornice and broken pillar; Greek red, Laconian black, or the fragments of the *Lupis Ophites* of Thebes, resembling the green of serpent scales heaped about the threshold where Pliny the Younger received his friends. His voice is an echo: "Be welcome, all, at this last hour of the day, when the sun slopes down the column of the Forum at Rome."

The bell in the fisherman's boat, with the nets attached, rocked by the tide, vibrates softly like the echo of vanished years.

V

PLINY'S ROSE

THE tourist steps ashore from a passing steamer at Bellaggio on the summer morning, skirts the arcades of the picturesque town, and enters the narrow gate leading by a winding and steep path to the Villa Serbelloni on the height above.

He is the type of his class, — a small, supple, sun-burned man, clad in grey tweed, with dusty shoes, and bag and field-glass strapped over his shoulder. Reticent of speech, and wary as to companionship, he pursues his way steadily and conscientiously. He is ubiquitous. He may be met on the margin of the Rhone glacier, ice-axe in hand, or clambering up the chimney of a dolomite with equal probability, and lifts his hat to a fellow-traveller in either locality, as on the quay of Bellaggio, with his habitual, slight, dry smile.

A World's Shrine

The Villa Serbelloni is a world's rendezvous as well as the terraces of Monte Carlo. Least like the modern hotel of all caravansaries, one never knows what eminent personage, diplomatic, princely, or ecclesiastical will emerge from a long casement, shaded by awning or shutter, or be encountered in the rambling corridors of the old mansion. Matchless in situation is this shrine of beauty, with blooming terraces sloping down to Lake Lecco on one side, the tranquil expanse of Como on the other, and facing all that wonderland of mountain amphitheatre, capped by the snowy pinnacles of the Splügen range, and coloured by the richest hues of Nature's palette in the changes from light to shade of the passing hours.

If the tourist is inspired by curiosity in his fellow-creatures, he pauses, seats himself at a table, and orders wine and a seltzer siphon of a nimble menial. He scans the dark individual escorted by two companions of respectful mien, who is possibly a prime minister in search of repose. The lady with red hair and a hard-favoured

Pliny's Rose

physiognomy is, at the very least, a grand-duchess, travelling incognita. He need experience no surprise if a Siamese ambassador, in national costume, should stroll through the portico, and an Indian prince pause to light his cheroot at his elbow. Such great folk like the masquerade of losing personality in the crowd of common mortals, even as the unfortunate Empress of Austria is reputed to have bought the tickets on the steamers of Switzerland.

The probability is that the tourist shuns such company, and wanders through the gardens at will, pausing entranced at opportune points to enjoy the vistas chosen by modern taste and traditional usage. The familiar combination of natural loveliness and the artificial is more apparent on the promontory than elsewhere. The tourist has reached the goal of many an air-castle in journeys traced on the map of his guide-book, but all the drop-curtains and stage scenery of the theatres seem to have been borrowed from the spot in tinsel and pasteboard. The scene is a stage. Who knows if the great lady, with the

A World's Shrine

auburn locks, poses, and is writing a diary of travel to be published for the edification and delight of her subjects? May not the prime minister be rehearsing an address to a discontented province, as he paces the path? The Siamese should advance to the footlights, and sing a comic song from an operetta.

The hot sun already smites the glowing rock of promontory. The flowers droop parched and languid, the zones of aloe, lemon, and chrysanthemum of path and parterre. The tourist finds a nook still fragrant and dewy with the freshness of early morning on the brink of the crag, with the meeting-place of the waters far below. He throws himself down on the bank, presses his hat over his eyes, and clasps his hands above his head with a sigh of contentment. A glimpse of sky of the purest sapphire hue is visible through the delicate meshes of foliage of adjacent trees, and a mist of blue lake occasionally unfolds, when the branches sway in the breeze. His thoughts stray idly to the warfare waged here in the middle ages, when some valiant Baron for-

Pliny's Rose

tified the tongue of land as a strategic point of vantage against the raids of pirates and marauders, the bands of armed men of the fourteenth century belonging to the clans from the side of Menaggio or Varenna. He might spin a verse in his own language on the cruel dame with troublesome lovers, who had them flung over this brink.

He has entered the domain of the rose, and other impressions fade as his gaze rests on the flower. Elsewhere the gardener has devised every artifice of bower, trellis, and parterre for the annuals, and perennials, the begonias, gladiolus, irides, poppies, spiræ, cystus, or carnations, but the rose reigns in this nook. The rose belonged to the Roman garden, laid out in stiff, geometrical forms, with the shrubbery clipped in the semblance of ships, urns, and such animals as bears holding a snake in the mouth, arbours, covered paths, and spaces in the borders for flowers, the Violaria and Rosaria of somewhat sparse adornment.

"Pliny's little rose of Como," muses the tourist in recognition.

A World's Shrine

He is a dreamer on this spot. Who is not? The perfume of the rose permeates all his senses, a soft medium of colour, creamy and pink, envelopes the dell in a warm atmosphere.

The promontory of Bellaggio is supposed to have been the site of Pliny's Villa of Tragedy. On such a height were constructed pavilion, portico, gallery, the hot and cold bath, the broad alley of the Hippodrome for exercise, the calorifere hidden in the walls to temper the first chill of winter. From the portals of Tragedy Pliny gazed on the sparkling waters, and the boats of the fishermen with sails spread, shining in the warm sunshine. All about him were those elements of life dear to the country gentleman. He might cultivate paternal lands with his own oxen, watch the shearing of sheep, prune vines, graft pears, and gather grapes. His garners were enriched with olives and grain. The elm-tree was clothed with vines, and the oak yielded abundant acorns for the cattle. The verdant gloom of thickly mantling ivy shielded the ledges where the narcissus was steeped in dew, the golden crocus

Bellaggio

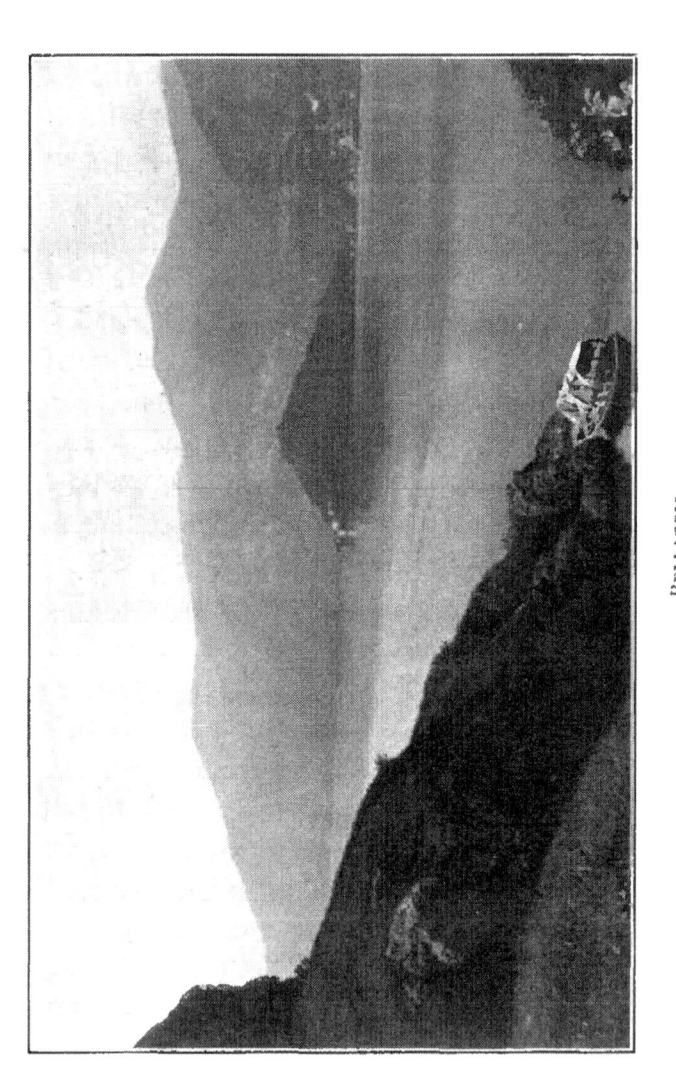

Pliny's Rose

awoke with the spring, and the lily rose stiffly on its green stalk, with alabaster cup permeated by a tremulous light, and yellow corolla hidden deep in the exquisite chalice. Topiarius, the gardener, planted laurel, taxus, cyprus, myrtle, rosemary, arches of evergreen, and margins of bearsfoot.

Estimating him by other traits of character the inference is clear that the mild and benevolent Pliny was kind to animals, and cherished such pets in this ideal retreat as monkeys, magpies, harmless snakes, ichneumons, and cats. We might almost infer that he was capable of becoming one of those ancients inclined to refrain from slaying beast, bird, or fish, as early vegetarians, and precursors of the advocates of suppression of cruelty.

Did night bring to the pillow of Pliny on the height the sound sleep so highly prized by the Roman? Calm yet sleepless he may have sought for new methods of enlightenment for his contemporaries as to many mysteries hidden from view, like Lucretius, until the dawn broke, and he went forth to inhale the fresh air from the hills

A World's Shrine

beyond Lecco. Time swayed his sceptre over the Villa of Tragedy. One marvels as to the methods adopted of noting the passing hours. At least Pliny, reared by his worthy uncle, did not seek to kill time. Rather would he grasp the mysterious power, without objective existence, by the wings as it rushed past. The early Phœnician did not require to warn the Plinys that time is precious; time is gold-dust, elephant's-teeth, and ostrich-plumes. Life is short.

The flowers possibly served as a clock on the heights to Pliny the Younger. Kindred blossoms did the work of four-o'clock, the portulaca of noon, the niotago of five, the geranium of six, and the evening primrose, cacti, moon-flower, chicory, sow-thistle, or dandelion. The rose grew here then, and greeted Pliny when he sallied forth to enjoy his domain. Campanian and Præstine, earliest and latest in bloom, cousin of the winter bud of the mountain slopes about Lugano, and equally related to the famous flowers of Pæstum, the harvest brought to Rome from Egypt in cold weather, Milesian, damask,

Pliny's Rose

rosa lutea, or *centifolia*, the rose is still sovereign, and suffers no change of fashion, like the abashed fuchsia, obliged to trail lovely sprays in neglected spots. Even now the gardener, Topiarius, when weary of fresh experiments in grafting, roots, and seed sowing, of crotons or orchids, to produce eccentric result of combination, turns to the rose to enrich in tints and fragrance. Once rose oil and rose ointment were used as medicaments here, as well as adopted in Roman cookery, the Persians and Arabs having taught Europe to distil flowers.

Hot sunshine encroaches on cool shadows. The echo of Pliny's words recurs to somnolent idleness:

"It is noon. At Rome the sun is watched by the accensus of the consuls between the old Rostra and the Græcostasis."

The tourist consults his watch, gazes down through the network of foliage at the lake and the boats with sails set, and returns to the prosaic world once more.

Pleasure is the flower that fades; remembrance is the lasting perfume.

VI

AT THE SPRING

ON a summer afternoon the bark of Memory was freighted with a gay company intent on visiting the gushing source of the spring rendered celebrated by Pliny the Younger, and which still flows and ebbs through all the years. The light craft carried beauty, fashion, art, and learning over the lake, with laughter, jest, and song to the gates of the Villa Pliniana, the gloomy palace at Palanzo at the base of the cliff. Here Pliny invoked Sylvanus, reposed on the grass beside the fountain, and listened to the birds. He judged that a portion of ground not over large, a spring, and a little woodland sufficed for the wants of man.

The party was not composed of such elements as the Arcadians of the seventeenth century of

At the Spring

Rome, who repaired to the hills to read sonnets, elegies, canzonets, and epigrams. They had no guide, Ciampoli, Crescimbeni, or Metastasis, adopted by Gravina among the guests, yet each prepared to enjoy the hour in a characteristic fashion. They sought the rocky portal of the spring, and the practical element unpacked the hampers on a convenient space of green sward. The tragedienne cast aside the fatigues of a professional career in all European capitals with her straw hat on the ground, and pushed back the coronet of heavy, black, braided hair from a fine brow. Beauty, very tiny and piquante, essayed on tiptoe to drag down some sprays of ivy from a wall.

"The most precious perfumes are ever kept in the smallest vases," said the French composer, gallantly assisting in the task.

"Pour libations to Ceres that the wheat may grow for all this countryside!" exclaimed the poet of the hour with mock fervour. "Bring wine, roses, nard, and meats for the sacrifice to this shrine of Pliny's meditations." He was

A World's Shrine

esteemed himself an amiable pagan, who believed in Pales, Venus, and still more firmly in the Muses.

The historian, tall, slender, with the severe features and silvered locks of a sage, was the chosen host of the occasion. His creed in an illustrious career was that truth was the polar star of his navigation.

"What shall the meats of sacrifice be, my friend?" he demanded, smiling.

"The picnic is ancient," said the American. "In the time of Tertullian each of us would have brought his own plate."

"As to food, Achilles received Priam with lamb, and bread served in baskets," suggested the Tragedienne, helping herself to fruit.

"Homer praised flour mingled with cheese and honey as the most delicate portion of heroes," added the English geologist.

"A fig for Homer!" railed the poet. "I scorn, to-day, even Pliny's thrushes, served with wild asparagus cut under the vines. Give me nothing less than the brains of the six ostriches

At the Spring

on a silver dish demanded by Heliogabalus. Well! If needs must—" and he removed a ham-sandwich, with finger and thumb, from a pyramid heaped on a napkin.

The lady of rank nibbled a galette, while the sunshine sparkled on the jewels in her ears and on her hands.

"For whom do you weave a garland?" she inquired of Beauty.

The latter had gathered her harvest of ivy sprays in her lap, and sat in the shade of the laurel hedge, a charming figure enveloped in silky draperies and lace.

"I must choose a subject," she replied demurely, surveying her companions through her eyelashes.

"Ah!" sighed the French composer. "Lucullus paid a thousand crowns for the portrait of Glycera seated, and making a flower wreath."

"My child, it is easier to fashion a garland than to find a head worthy to wear it, according to Goethe," warned the historian.

Whereupon Beauty approached, and dropped

A World's Shrine

her crown on his silvery locks, amidst the applause of her friends.

The singers, soprano and tenor, paced the path slowly, arm in arm, their voices blending in a subdued and fragmentary cadence. The Swede dislodged a fragment of stone from an archway with his cane. He discussed the possibility of a glacier origin, and how it came there, with the Englishman and American. Truly science has no country, and the trio were brothers on the spot. The Frenchman held a wine-glass of foaming Asti, and demanded of the bevy of ladies, in the language of Charles d'Orléans, the Beranger of the fifteenth century, in what country the beautiful Flora was to be discovered, the discreet Héloïse, the white Queen Blanche, like a lily, who sang with the voice of a siren, or Jeanne, the good Lorrainese burned by the English at Rouen.

"Sacrilege!" quoth the American, approaching the fount with a cup. "Pliny should be pledged in his spring here, at least."

"To the fountain of Bandusium as clear as glass, and the source where Numa sacrificed a

At the Spring

kid crowned with flowers," echoed the Swede, filling a crystal goblet in turn. "To the first temperance man, Lycurgus, King of Thrace, who had the vines in his kingdom uprooted because his subjects were becoming too fond of the fermented juice," said the diplomatist from the Hague.

"Bacchus made him mad in revenge," added the lady of rank, slyly, and dipped her jewelled fingers in the rill.

"Sheer fallacies!" interposed the poet, mutinously, and uncorked a bottle of champagne. "Pliny recommended old Falernian, poured in bowls and cooled in a stream."

"Assuredly," assented the diplomatist. "Also the lyrics of Alcæus were drinking-songs in praise of wine, which never came amiss, apparently, in the heat of summer, the cold of winter, the blazing dogstar, and driving tempest."

"I must declare with Tony Lumpkin, that good liquor gives genius a better discerning," said the Englishman, replenishing his glass with sherry.

A World's Shrine

The tragedienne quoted Cassio: "O thou invisible spirit of wine, if thou hast no name to be known by let us call thee devil."

The traveller readjusted his fez, and ate a slice of melon with gravity.

"The Koran hath it that every berry of the vine is a devil," he supplemented.

The American insisted, with Longfellow, that youth dwells in the fountains, the rivulets from the hills, and not in casks and cellars.

Silence ensued, a lull of mere chat in the languid heat, like the effervescence of the liquid in the half-emptied glass, and the fragments of the repast scattered on the sward.

Pliny, the host, once more spoke in his letter to Licinius Surra:

"I have brought you a little gift from my native place in the shape of a problem quite worthy of your profound knowledge. A spring rises in the mountain, runs down among the rocks, and is received in an artificial chamber where one can lunch. After a short stay there it falls into the Lake of Como. Its character is extraordinary. Three times a day it waxes and

At the Spring

wanes with regular rise and fall. That is plain to be seen, and is very interesting to watch. You lie near to it, and eat your food, while you drink from the spring itself, which is intensely cold. Meanwhile it either ebbs or flows with sure and measured movements. Suppose you place a ring, or anything else you like, upon a dry spot. The water reaches it and at last covers it, again slowly retires and leaves the object bare. If you watch longer you may see this double process repeated a second and a third time. Can it be that some subtle wind alternately opens and shuts the mouth and jaws of the spring, as it rushes in and out again? Or is the nature of the ocean the nature of this spring, as well? On the same principle that the former ebbs and flows does this modest stream experience its alternate tides? Or, as rivers which run into the sea are hurled back by counter winds and incoming currents, so is there something which checks the flow of this spring?"

The shadows of the trees deepened with the waning afternoon. The house gleamed mute and cold through the foliage. Associations of conspiracy, gloomy failures, and tragic revelations of state secrets seem to belong to the spot, as the

A World's Shrine

moss and ivy cling to the masonry. The villa was built by the Count Giovanni Anguissola, one of the four assassins of the Duke Farnese at Piacenza. A transient bloom of feminine loveliness and grace gleams here, for a moment, in the remembrance of the Princess Belgiojoso, patriotic heroine, diplomatic emissary, or political spy in the national affairs of her day, according to the point of view.

The shade of the chestnut groves of the upper slopes lengthened to the lake margin, and the company prepared to depart. The American, the water drinker of the party *par excellence*, filled a tiny cup of chamois horn at the spring, as a rite of farewell.

"A deep-seated reservoir, fed by perennial springs, and connected with the outer air by some syphon-like channel in the rock would solve the mystery of Pliny's fountain," he mused.

The English geologist held his hands in the cool current.

"Yes, there are intermittent wells in other lands," he assented.

At the Spring

"But with no such regularity of rise and fall," said the historian, eagerly.

The poet drew the Swede to a crevice of the rocks to listen to sounds which might be only the wind sighing through cavities and fissures, or the mysterious mingling of the voices of invisible beings.

"How truly does poetry become a science of life and of the human heart in such a place," he said. "Oh, what colouring it imparts to the passing hours! What delicacy of touch is needful on the flute of Arcady, the guitar of Provence, and the lyre!"

The French composer lighted a cigar and blew a cloud in the air.

"Renown is a puff of smoke, but Pliny seems to have enjoyed a fair share of it," he suggested. "Lucan celebrated in verse the citizen of the world, the man who does not consider himself born for his own uses alone, but for the human race, and is animated by a sacred love for the entire universe," remarked the historian, removing the ivy crown from his head, with a glance at Beauty.

A World's Shrine

"That description might serve as a portrait of Pliny the Younger," said the tragedienne, rising.

Where are they now, the company of a summer day? They haunt the shores of Como no more.

VII

A TEMPLE OF JUPITER

THE round temple, with roof supported by columns, was only a dilapidated summer house, by day, sadly in need of cement and whitewash. The battered statue on a pedestal in the centre might have represented Neptune, or Esculapius, as well as Jove. The property had been neglected since the decease of the last owner. Nature had made herself self-elected guardian of the stretch of shore in a tangled wilderness of roses and jasmine, brambles and weeds, stifling the mildewed busts and nymphs flanking the path leading to the temple in the embrace of rank vines, and untrimmed shrubbery.

Youth had ridiculed these goddesses, with all the garish blemishes wrought by Time unveiled in the morning light, and even sketched carica-

A World's Shrine

tures of such as lacked noses, an arm, or had fallen prone among the geraniums of the border. Youth escaped as evening deepened to night from the crowded table d'hôte, sought the secluded temple, seated himself on the step, and kindled a fresh cigarette. The beautiful girl opposite at dinner had strolled away with the officer afterward. Youth, gifted with the extraordinary volubility of his years, and the Latin races, had discussed the religions of the world with his elders. He was alert to take a part in this age of eternal inquiry, philosophical or religious. Should he adhere to a stoicism merging into Jansenism and Calvinism; Epicureanism, contented with a flowery surface of things; a Pantheism that adores to the depths; or the Deism which finds the universe full of beneficent sunshine? Lo! the lore of the universities of Bologna, Pisa, and Rome was on his lips. His mother had listened to his prating with complacency. The beautiful girl, femininely inconsequent, had lent ear to the airy badinage of the military hero instead.

A Temple of Jupiter

The student was a prey to novel emotions, the unfolding of manhood in the "vernal impulsion that makes lyrical all that hath language." He sought the solitude of the neglected garden to avoid mere noisy companionship, and listen to the nightingales reputed to haunt these thickets. Physical twilight is precious to all souls at times, according to Pater. The reclining nymph on the ledge held her broken urn, and the water flowed into a moss-stained basin below, with a gurgling, monotonous rhythm of sound. The nightingale poured forth a sudden, gushing melody from the foliage, at once melancholy and rich. The cigarette smoke became a white cloud, and touched his eyelids. The flowing water, and the nightingale's note mingled in a blended undertone. Surely the shapes about stirred, the smoke was swept hither and thither into the semblance of a dancing movement of satyrs and naiads wending through the shrubbery. A range of rudely cut heads on a coping near the ground, which were sufficiently coarse to belong to the earthen vases of clay of the age of Numa, laughed. They were the little gods down among the roots and turf.

"We belong to the most ancient forms of worship, Greek, Assyrian, and Indian," they seemed to clamour. "Make sacrifice to us with cakes and crackling salt! Pour libations of wine about the plane tree!"

A bust on a pillar near-by announced reproachfully to the mortal intruder:

"You drew my profile to-day with a broken chin. I am not a boy, but a girl. I am Juventas, the Hebe of the Greeks. I am Youth. I wish to know, to understand all! My brain teems with many projects of enterprise."

"Child! How you prattle on," remarked the seated Jove.

In the dusk this shrine was blanched to marble and pearl. Jupiter, from whom mankind once received all blessings and misfortunes, held his sceptre of cypress and the thunderbolts, while his throne was made of ivory and gold. On Como the god may have taught the first man to eat acorns from the oak-tree sacred to him.

A Temple of Jupiter

Even sacrifice of the bull, with gilded horns, and a garland of roses around the neck, by white-robed priests, might have taken place before this altar, while saffron was cast on the fire.

The student, seated on the step, longed to inquire if this was the statue placed in the Temple of Jupiter by Pliny the Younger when he returned to Como in maturity, but his lips were dumb.

"I have my own thoughts," protested Juventas.

"It is enough to live through the summer hours, with pipe of flute and dancing," said Faunus from the ilex hedge.

"No! It is not enough," retorted Juventas.

"My very words at table," thought the student. "How this battered head interprets my own opinions."

A murmur of kindred voices was audible from the adjacent path.

"What do you wish to know?"

"The creeds of men. The true religion through all ages," replied rash adolescence.

"Child, seek not to be overwise," admonished Jupiter, as if weary of his power.

A World's Shrine

"Just pipe and dance with the nymphs as befits your years," mocked Faunus.

The voices in the alley increased in animation, oddly mingled with the gurgling flow of water from the broken urn, and an occasional outburst of song of the nightingale. There seemed to be endless discussion of dimly conceived personification of benignant deities, to be propitiated, of the mysteries of a future life, and the demigods to bridge over the chasm between mortality and the realm of spirits in the fear of Minos and Cerberus. One voice spoke distinctly of the gloomy tenets of the Etruscans, the mysticism of Asia, the genial mythology of Greece.

"Which to believe?" sighed Juventas.

"Believe in life and happiness," said Faunus, carelessly. "Let Venus make her *parure* of myrtle, and the naiads deck themselves with pale violets. Leave the laurel to Apollo. Gather narcissus and tufts of aniseed."

Ceres, matronly and benign, guarded a ruined fountain, with a shrine near-by which might have

A Temple of Jupiter

belonged to the Lares and Penates, adorned with a bunch of poppies.

"Mine is the true religion," she said, musingly. "Worship all nature in the bounty of the gifts of seed-time and harvest."

"Ah, Mother Earth, it does not suffice for the human soul to reap and sow," said Socrates from the shrubbery. "Men are not all early farmers. Keep your Penates for rustic hearths and the corner shrines of Roman streets."

"The Christian poet, Prudentius, even complained of genii, symbols, and portraits over baths and houses, with wax candles and lanterns hung before tutelary deities," meditated the student.

"I will study and reflect night and day until I find the clue I seek," demurred Juventas.

"Eat, drink, and be merry," counselled Faunus.

Aphrodite, among the roses, laughed.

"Much learning of books may make you mad," reasoned Faunus, lightly.

"All men are a little mad," affirmed Zeno, in the distance.

A World's Shrine

"I must win honour and fame in my time," cried Juventas.

"Child, you have projects enough in your mind for a thousand years," said Jupiter, gravely.

"Beloved Pan, and all ye other gods who haunt this place, give beauty in the inward soul, and may the outward and inward be one," exclaimed Socrates.

Then Epictetus spoke sweetly in protest of materialism, and for a striving after noble aims and mental tranquillity. In the first century the Stoics and Epicureans had essayed to supply a rule of life which they could not find in the worship of the gods.

"Ah, well! We are all brothers because we are all God's children," concluded the philosopher.

After that it seemed to the student all debate was fragmentary and confusing among the philosophers of the shrubbery. He became aware, with a thrill of wonder, that the Flora, in her light tunic, resembled the beautiful girl of his thoughts, and was actually the presiding presence of the neglected parterre.

A Temple of Jupiter

"Cold is mitigated by the Zephyrs. Summer follows close upon the spring, shortly to die itself, as soon as fruitful autumn shall have shed its fruits, and anon sluggish winter returns again," Flora murmured.

The note of a bell fell on the ear of the student. He started to his feet. The cigarette had fallen on the ground. The statues were mute. The nightingale was hushed, and the water flowed from the urn monotonously. The bell pealed out on the darkness from a church tower, ringing the Ave Maria an hour before dawn of the June day. Thus the Christian sect, tolerated as inoffensive and unimportant by the Emperor Trajan and Pliny the Younger, has grown through all the succeeding centuries and spread to the ends of the earth.

VIII

SIGNAL TOWERS

LIVES there a traveller journeying towards Lake Como who is not moved to an awakening curiosity and interest by the first glimpse of a tower rising on a height? The adjacent detached fragments of masonry may suggest only the picturesque remnants of a mediæval castle, but the tower is a key-note, in site and foundations, at least, of the day of Roman ascendency over Europe. A picture of the romantic era of literature is presented to the most practical mind in the gliding past of a railway train, of the knight spurring forth over the drawbridge, falcon on wrist, and the noble dame in damask robe and farthingale at the casement. The tower, whether built of roughly jointed stone, with bold machicolations of battlements, or as having square angle turrets, has other associations.

Signal Towers

The tap of the telegraph is audible on the shores of Como to-day. The official in the station writes off the brief message, and sends forth the despatch to the local silk merchant, or the stranger within the gates. The transaction is scarcely of more moment than the arrival of the mail.

Once the towers on the ridge served the same end in a more tragic and momentous fashion. How thrilling the greeting, or warning, read by trembling women and children in the beacon of day or night from these signal stations! How the bronzed cheek of manhood paled, and the heart of youth throbbed tumultuously at the message that there was danger in the very air for all the inhabitants of the surrounding country, and even the frontier!

Now these citadels may be the granary of a farm, heaped full of hay and golden straw, with red peppers and ears of maize strung above an embrasure to dry in the sun of autumn. The pigeons circle around the parapet, and the swallows dart out of the fissures in the coping. In the court-yard and moat the fowls cackle, a

A World's Shrine

lamb bleats, or a donkey brays. The large square villa near-by has been the summer home for generations of a Lombard family. All wears the aspect of rural contentment and peace.

The old towers, furrowed and scarred by storms, guard their memories of a grim past.

Baradello on the hill of San Martino sent messages to Torno, Argegno, Cavagnola, Val Intelvi, Bellaggio, Valassina, Menaggio, Grandola, Rezzonico, and Torre Olinio to the Valtellina, on one side, and along the course of the Ticino, Chiasso, Mendrisio, and Bellinzona, with the three old castles still crowning the crags, on the other. These signals were colours by day, and torches, or bonfires on the highest peaks at night.

"The robber lord of yonder fastness is making ready to sally forth on a raid. Flee to shelter with the family and the flocks!" the warning of noon and night have been.

One hamlet could transmit the dreaded news to another in the gorges of the mountains by confiding several handfuls of sawdust to the rapid glacier stream to be swept on the current, and

Signal Towers

discerned by anxious eyes aware of the meaning. The beacon fire of midnight signified, possibly, a general alarm in the approach of vast armies of barbarians, fierce and strange of garb and speech, Goth, Gaul, and Hun intent on reaching the gates of Rome.

"Woe and desolation! The foe is upon us!" the pulsing flame of the hill-top proclaimed, and was answered by a wail of distress and fear throughout the length and breadth of the land.

And the old towers brood over the past. The present time does not touch them. The modern world moves on wings of light and speed in the telegraph, and on wings of sound in the telephone. The pigeons and swallows that build their nests under the battlements do not trouble their heads about the matter, unless they promise to carry a greeting to the next castle ruin in a fresh flight. The sheep and calves bleat below. Children laugh. A young *contadino* sings in a reedy voice, with curious turns and inflections of measure that severe cold in January, bad weather in February, wind in March, soft rains of April,

A World's Shrine

dews in May, a good reaping in June, a fine winnowing in July, and the three storms of August, — make a season worth more than the throne of Solomon.

An army in glittering uniform, with cavalry and artillery, capable of shattering any structure to the foundations with shell, or riddling the walls with bullets, does not disturb these hoary sentinels. The towers dote and dream only of those earlier hosts that advanced in slow waves of humanity, with their households, chariots, and weapons, and the murmur of many voices, even as the locusts settled on Lombardy in 873, and again in 1364, leaving no green leaf.

Pliny the Younger, as child and man, must have scanned the towers, demanding of these guardians if all was well, and the good citizens of Como might hope to sleep in security through the watches of the night. What would he have thought of that key-note of the twentieth century, whispering a message over the ocean wave, wireless telegraphy?

IX

AN ANCHORITE

MANY years ago a man climbed to the summit of Monte Generoso, and built himself some sort of hut, or rude chapel to dwell there. The act was more of an achievement than it is in our day, when the pedestrian who has descended to Como by that northern gate of mountain barrier takes a morning walk on the gentle slopes leading to the height, scornful of aid to vigorous muscles of funicular railway, or mule. The commonplace rite of seeking this renowned shrine to obtain the view cannot rob Nature of her charm of an unsurpassed richness and beauty in the spectacle of the amphitheatre of snow line visible, and the Lombardy plain stretching southward in billows of misty green verdure. Such

A World's Shrine

moments are, indeed, the very "peaks of life" to most mortals.

The pioneer climber was an anchorite, eager to plant his standard of Christianity on the crags. His personality is shadowy. His feat of making a hermit's cell on the top of a mountain, wherein to pray for the sins and sorrows of the world at his feet, seems one of unquestionable nobility of aim. He thus becomes the leading figure of the region in that dawning light of a new era of civilisation, with the sheltered, flower-scented haunts of the gods of Pliny's Eden of the lake below. The omens and oracles of pagan times had given way to visions ecstatic of the soul and conscience. The hermit dwelt in the shadow of the Past, in day-dreams, yet with fresh invocation of saints and worship of relics. The heathen turned away from death and sadness. Mediævalism meditated from preference on the charnel-house. What was gained without some loss in the example of the anchorite? He was not a San Abbondio, patron of that portion of Italy, whose history as fourth Bishop of Como, under Pope Leo I., and

An Anchorite

zeal in extirpating idolatry, may be read on the painted glass of the windows of the Como Cathedral. The miracles surrounding the name of St. Ambrose, as one of the Latin fathers, do not seem to have fallen to his share as well. He did not command a flock of geese to follow him into the presence of the Pope, like St. Leopardo, or call a company of birds to descend from the air, after the example of St. Brandolino. His name was Manfredo da Settala, and he was a Milanese by birth. As first curate of Cuazzo he was urged to pray at the tomb of San Gerardo at Monza that a visitation of pestilence at Olgiate might cease. The plague was stayed. The inference is clear that he had a reputation for sanctity from this fact.

The new creed acquired many picturesque phases around the Lake of Como with the lapse of years. The Lombardy plain was then a vast solitude, partially overflowed by rivers in spring and autumn, with thickets kept as preserves of hunting by the feudal lords. The peasantry were forbidden to poach on the pheas-

A World's Shrine

ants and hares, even if the harvest had been spoiled. Wild boars roamed in these woods even in the day of Francesco Sforza. The anchorite of Monte Generoso had outspread before him such a savage waste, instead of the blooming expanse now yielding grain, oil, chestnuts, and wine. The maize rippling in the yellow waves of a golden sea beneath the rays of the fierce July and August sun, was brought from Soria during the Crusades; a royal gift to Italy. The slave populations of Rome planted the first gardens around Como, but agriculture owed much to the early monks, who everywhere cleared forests, made the morass fertile, and cultivated vines and olives. The most ancient archives contain records of kitchen gardens, meadows, orchards, groves, vineyards, pasturage, and aqueducts. Pious ladies acquired the agreeable custom of bestowing property on religious communities. In 757, Valderana, wife of Arochis da Arzago made a gift to the church of San Zenone in Campione, with land, olives, and vineyards. The holy William of Monza built a Franciscan

An Anchorite

monastery above Como. Elena de Pedragli erected a convent at Brunate in 1341. The thought is harmonious that the monks may have introduced many plants, brought by pilgrims and travellers from distant lands, acacia, red oak, clover, the locust tree to sustain slips of the mountains, and the border of torrents, the meadow lupine of arid and calcareous districts, the agave and heath. The monastery of San Abbondio became noted for serving the trout of the Adda and Poschieva, streams still famous for these fish. The cheese of Ardenno and Berbenno acquired reputation, as well as the olives and mills. The good cheer and hospitality of the abbeys of all countries is suggested by the praise of the unusual size of some truffles sent by St. Felix, first Bishop of Como, to St. Ambrose in early annals.

The record of religious orders for six centuries is that of the preservation of learning, building churches, working in mosaic, carving wood, painting glass, and establishing laboratories of drugs and chemicals. Spiritual-minded women

A World's Shrine

became abbesses and saints all about the lake of Como, as in England and Germany, emulative of Elisabeth of Hungary, Hildegarde, and Walpurga. None of them obtained the celebrity of a Catherine of Siena, or St. Theresa. The order of the Umiliati established the manufacture of wool in Lombardy. Women, especially nuns, spun, and men wove white robes and veils.

The anchorite watched and prayed instead. In the twilight his image is readily fashioned out of the gathering clouds and shadows, as certain rocks of the Carrara mountains gain a human semblance of a giant, or a spirit of the Apennines, winged and bearded, and a crag beyond Mentone is the figure of a monk seated, with his head enveloped in a cowl. If accurate history of the recluse of Monte Generoso has been treasured in monastic archives, and saints' lives, the research is beyond our ken. What manner of holy man was he? How did he live on the summit? Did the country folk bring him offerings of food, as the bowl of the Eastern fakir is filled with rice by the faithful? His fare may have been herbs

An Anchorite

and roots. A faithful goat possibly accompanied him to this retreat to nourish the recluse with rich milk, and subsist on the scanty herbage among the broom of the belt above chestnut and beech-wood. The cattle that browse on the slopes through the summertide, with a melodious tinkle of bells, and thrust the innocent heads of pretty heifers, confidingly, on pedestrians sketching in nooks, can scarcely have obtained a footing in the thickets at that date. The bees, clad in brown velvet waistcoats, buzzed about other blooms than the great, silvery thistles of the August noon, the gentian of high pastures, flax, thyme, or madder. He left to the communities of the valleys labour, and chose contemplation. Expiation for the crimes of war, penances, martyrdom would have served the aim of seeking such a goal. If he adhered to the mystic tenets of St. Francis he scourged himself, imagined that he was tormented by demons in the vigils of night, or indulged in visions of a Heaven peopled with angels. If he was a follower of St. Benedict his hours were spent in calm

A World's Shrine

meditation. We like to consider him as a sort of Friar Laurence, going forth at break of day with his osier basket to gather baleful weeds and precious-juiced flowers, finding within the infant rind of one tiny blossom that poison had residence, and medicine power, and moralising on similar good and evil principles in man. Ready was he, also, to dip into tragedies of life, and heal strife. He chose the light. He had eyes and a soul. If his senses were benumbed by years and suffering, his perceptions blurred by the morbid and fantastic doctrines of his fellow-man, how can it have been otherwise? His nature must have become luminous with the glowing universe surrounding him.

He watched the East with folded hands, after the gloom of awful engulfing darkness, when the stars paled, and one by one the mountains grew distinct from Monte Viso to the Bernina, the crown-like head of Monte Rosa, the chalky white masses of Mont Blanc, and the sharp and jagged outline of the Bernese oberland. The sky became tinged with lilac, purple, and crimson as

An Anchorite

the rising sun touched the peaks with a spear of fire. Far below the lakes reflected the heavens, Varese, Maggiore, Lugano, with all the exquisite gradations of tints of a peacock's plumage, and Como a sheet of crystal.

The anchorite, as solitary spectator, gazed at these amplitudes of space, and praised his Creator.

X

A MEDIÆVAL QUEEN

ONCE upon a time there was a queen, and she made a journey in a litter to the mineral baths of Val Masino, in the Valtellina, along the *cornice* between Menaggio and Gravedona, leading from Como to Trepievi, known as the Queen's Road (*Strada Regina*) to this day. The cliff is precipitous, and of a tawny hue, hence the name of Orange Rock, and the path considered dangerous. The Russians chose the route in 1799, and many soldiers fell over the brink.

The flowers blooming in clefts of the roadside know all about the matter, from their ancestors, and the birds — such as escape from the snare of the fowler in these regions — have, no doubt, heard the tale from their feathered grandmothers of how Theodolinda, of wise and virtuous fame,

A Mediæval Queen

was an early traveller on these shores. One of the charms of the irregular growth of town, hamlet, or villa property of the little Paradise is that roads do not environ the lake in firm causeway or picturesque cornice, wending amidst the shrubbery, but intrude, for a span, in a casual mode, between promontory, bay, and mountain wall. The Queen's Road is therefore the more conspicuous. This noble lady lived a long time ago, having been born in the year 561, but her renown still endures. The Lombards held sway in Italy for two hundred and six years, until subdued by Charlemagne in 774. The dominion of Odoacer had extended from Sicily to the Danube. His wife, Andefleda, owned a palace on Como. Theodolinda is called a Lombard queen. She was a Bavarian princess. Her story is a romantic one. When Rosamund had slain her lord Alboin, with the aid of two officers, during his afternoon nap, for proffering her father's skull as a drinking-cup in tipsy jocularity, the Lombards gathered at Pavia to choose a new ruler. They presented the lance of command to Clefis, who governed them unwillingly for a year and a half, and was assassinated by a groom. The Lombard nobility next decided to elect a king, and chose his son, Autaris, "the long-haired," a youth of bravery and beauty. He sent an embassy to Garibaldo, King of Bavaria, demanding the hand of his daughter in marriage. He went himself as an adventurous knight on the mission, disguised as the emissary, to see the fair one and judge of her merit. Evidently this Longobard had all the sterling qualities of his race, deemed hard and rough by the softer and more flexible Southern character, and cherished other sentiments than those of conquest and bloodshed. Theodolinda, full of maidenly grace, according to the chivalrous chronicler, handed the nuptial wine-cup to her father's guest. The young pair exchanged a glance of sympathy, and he kissed her hand with ardour in saluting the chalice. Dazzled and confused, Theodolinda confided the matter to her nurse, and this sagacious foster-mother divined the personality of the suitor. One is reminded of pictures of the Dutch and Munich schools,

A Mediæval Queen

rich in sentiment and detail, with all the shimmer of gems, weapons, and polished platters, the attendants and strangers grouped in the background, and that central figure, the princess, with tresses braided down her back, presenting the goblet and meeting a lover's contemplation in the envoy.

Subsequently the Bavarian monarch fled to Verona with his child, to escape from disturbances in his kingdom, instigated by the Frank Chilperic of Soissons to prevent the union. Theodolinda married Autaris, who lived a year. She then espoused Agiluph, Duke of Turin, who became King of the Lombards in 590. He embraced the Catholic faith, as well as many of his nobles, through her influence, while civilisation among the Lombards is considered to have begun with him. She is reproached by some authorities for thus supplanting Autaris "before his ashes were cold." The times were critical, and the lady Theodolinda, as a widow, may have sadly needed masculine protection for her throne. She would seem to have been fortunate in her

A World's Shrine

choice of consorts; at least neither of them offered her King Garibaldo's head as a drinking-cup in gruesome fashion. Had they done so, possibly she would have known how to manage them. She belongs in tradition to the ranks of good queens, about whom homely tales linger in song and poetry with the country-folk, the Berthas and Clotildas. Born to the purple, she played the difficult rôle of sovereign in a creditable manner. We are familiar with Queen Bertha, twirling her distaff as she rode her palfrey, as an example to the idle women among her subjects. Queen Theodolinda is associated with her hen and seven chickens, wrought in gold, as symbolical of Lombardy and her seven provinces. She had two children, a son, Adaloardo, and a daughter, Gundeberga. The children were christened, and the Basilica built at Monza by the parents, dedicated to St. John Baptist, in honour of the event. Here the son was crowned in the presence of Theodolinda. Pope Gregory the Great sent congratulations on the birth of an heir, and presented the mother with the Iron Crown. Two other

A Mediæval Queen

coronets were kept in the treasury besides the circlet of iron. These were encrusted with jewels, and on one was engraved in Latin: "Agiluph, by the grace of God, a brave man, King of all Italy, makes this votive offering to San Giovanni in the Church of Monza." Theodolinda, during her reign, built a bridge of eighteen arches over the Breggia near Cernobbio; a fine Campanile in the Brianza San Giovanni di Besano, above Viggino; the Tower of Perledo; the Church of San Martino, near Varenna; and St. John at Gravedona, on the site of a temple of Apollo.

She passes no more along the Strada Regina of Como in her litter. For further trace of her we must seek the Monza Cathedral, with its ancient bas-reliefs over the western door, a Lombardo Gothic sanctuary built in the fourteenth century on the site of the earlier structure of 595. Here is the sarcophagus holding the ashes of Theodolinda, and all the record of her greatness. In the casket of the altar is the famous crown, lined with the iron made of a nail from the cross on Calvary, brought to Europe by the

A World's Shrine

Empress Helena, worn at the coronation of thirty-four Lombard kings, and fitted on the head of many a brilliant monarch since. In the treasury the hen still guards her chickens, executed by the order of the royal lady, and her fan and comb may be inspected.

Quaint, virile, and full of a certain dignity is the memory of the Mediæval Queen.

XI

A TINY GIBRALTAR

THE modern warrior was alone on the Island of San Giovanni, in the Tremezzina, that portion of the lake known as the garden of Lombardy. He was a quiet gentleman of simple habits, fond of children, and of gathering ferns. A close scrutiny of his lineaments disclosed neck, chin, and cheek tanned deep bronze by the African sun, and a scar across the forehead of grim aspect. He measured the islet with his footsteps, and traced the hint of walls, buttresses, and arches with his cane.

"A Gibraltar in miniature," he soliloquised, smilingly. "Why not?"

Then he seated himself on a rock, and crushed an aromatic plant beneath his shoe. A lizard

A World's Shrine

ran along a ledge, and paused on a stone to regard the intruder with true lizard curiosity. He avoided frightening the pretty creature by any brusque movement. He drew a note-book from his pocket.

"I wonder if I shall be arrested, as a spy, by the government of the country if I take down the form of this stronghold," he said; and his pencil idly traced imaginary turrets and bastions, while he mused on the history of the spot.

When the Emperor Justinian I. reigned at Constantinople, and his generals Belisarius and Narses had carried the fear of his arms into Persia and Africa, the latter conquered Italy. Lo! the Empress Sofia is said to have sneered at Narses, who, affronted, took a terrible revenge. The sway of the Goths had crumbled, and Totila been slain. Narses invited the Longobards into Italy to overthrow the power of the Eastern Empire. The fresh hordes, blue-eyed, and fierce, obeyed the summons. Alboin left Pannonia for Milan and Pavia. Such were the Lombards,

A Tiny Gibraltar

adhering to many ancient Germanic customs, sensitive to honour, and usually chivalrous in the protection of women, scorning all luxury, and their language a difficult dialect to the Italians. They had only one trade, as a nomadic race, that of war, held their laws solely by memory, were deemed very ignorant, not knowing how to read or write, and worshipped an idol made of the trunk of a tree. Discord had arisen among the Franks under Childipert. Autaris was made king in 584. Alboin, of cruel memory, had slain Cunemund of Servia, and forced his daughter Rosamund to marry him. Alboin turned his arms against the northern provinces of Italy, and gave the famous banquet at Verona in 573, when he invited his consort Rosamund to drink from her father's skull. Narses had everywhere cut the dikes of foreign invasion.

Twenty years before Alboin overran the land, the Governor Francillioni of Como retired to the little islet of Comacina, and began to fortify the place as a refuge. Timid folk flocked here in the hope that times would improve. Other cities deposited their riches within the walls for safe-keeping.

The island is half a mile long, and three hundred feet wide. It is situated in the Tremezzina of the lake, with the narrow stretch of water known as the Zocca del Olio separating it from the mainland. The dilapidated chapel of St. John alone remains. In the sixth century, at the date of the Lombard invasion, the stronghold decided to hold out against all foes, and still swear allegiance to the emperor at Constantinople. The historical fact is droll at this distance of time. An islet in the middle of a little lake building towers, and gates, and battlements, in defiance of all the powers of the vicinity, in fealty to a distant emperor. Consider the valour of these pygmy hosts! The garrison that manned the walls, the sentinels scanning adjacent shores, the guardians of the hoarded riches calculated to arouse the cupidity of barbarians, the discipline and vigilance essential in the heart of the citadel to suppress treachery and inspire courage — all had to be maintained with firmness. There was naval

THE COMACINA

A Tiny Gibraltar

warfare then! Autaris laid siege to the place with a mimic fleet and reduced it by famine in six months. The Governor Francillioni was able to secure honourable terms, and retired to Ravenna. The treasure fell to the enemy, precious vestments, jewels, money, chalices, and vessels of gold and silver once brought here by fugitives from their homes and churches.

After King Rotharis had codified the Lombard customs into laws, in 636, and established guilds and trades, the *Magistri Comacini* were guests on the island. These were local artisans and builders, and are known as the first freemasons. They built the Monza Cathedral. In architecture the Goths of the fifth century found in Italy the classical Roman debased. Enclesius, Bishop of Ravenna, visited Constantinople in the sixth century, and brought back Greek workers from St. Sofia to erect San Vitale. Roman and Byzantine blended in a third order of Romanesque, or Comacine.

The warlike spirit of the people of the island was not subdued. In the political disturbances

A World's Shrine

of succeeding years, when the towns on the lake were divided by factions, the Comacina played a part in sieges and defiances of all sorts. In the contentions of Milan and Como of the middle ages, the tiny Gibraltar is reputed to have rebelled at maternal authority for ten years in favour of the rival. In wrath Como sent her fleet to punish the culprit. The rallying and setting sail of the war ships must have been an awe-inspiring spectacle from the shores of the lake. Forth sallied the Cristina, the Rat, the Griffin, the Wolf. Each of these had a wooden tower, while other craft were furnished with machines for firing stones, arrows, and combustibles. A galley was long and heavy enough to transport projectiles of war, and another boat noted for speed. A captain at arms of Gravedona had invented *lo Schifo* in this bellicose era; a bark holding twelve rowers, and twelve soldiers ready for action, with a white gonfalone with the three red crosses of the parish on it at the masthead, a crucifix and an altar on the deck. The island strengthened the fortifications which covered the

A Tiny Gibraltar

place in stubborn resistance. Ah, hunger might be warded off for a season, and clumsy implements thunder at gate and tower in vain; even soldier in cuirass and helmet meet hostile soldier with clash of steel in some feat of sallying forth to the fray, but the day came when battlement and buttress would fall, like a house of cards, before a more formidable foe than the Lombard hosts, or mediæval armies. Gunpowder came into general use. The sceptre of the islet passed. Gunpowder slew its thousands, and enabled the middle classes to cope with the knight in armour.

Delécluze affirms that disputes as to the form of the earth caused Columbus to cross the Atlantic; and the mechanical implements, simple toys of children, of the thirteenth century, were the first models of artillery destined to change the politics of Europe.

The lizards crept away among the tufts of grass and vines. The waters sparkled in a flood of sunshine. It might be better for the world if no more trace existed of the great

A World's Shrine

fortifications, Quadrilateral, Ehrenbretstein, Gibraltar, and the modern warrior, so skilful with flashing sabre on occasion, wielded only his cane or umbrella of a summer holiday on Como.

XII

A SPORTSMAN OF THE MIDDLE AGES

THE rise of the Visconti to sovereign power in the thirteenth century furnished a phase of surpassing richness in the development of civilisation. Splendour, tyranny, cruelty, and deadly treachery were combined in these princes in a manner quite unparalleled in European history. Como was ever at the mercy of the despots, with other towns.

Bernarbò Visconti, born in 1319, stepped upon the scene as master of Bergamo, Brescia, Crema, and Cremona, one of the three nephews who succeeded Giovanni, Archbishop of Milan. Audacious and brutal, Bernarbò was excommunicated by the Pope Urban V., who preached a crusade against him, and sought to crush the culprit by means of the Emperor Charles IV. He was a keen sportsman, and fond of tracking the wild boar with dogs. He was severe with all poachers on his preserves, and is accused of having them tortured, burned, or slain. He had the Abbot of St. Barnaba hung for taking hares. His enemies stigmatised him as a Nero, or a Caligula. That he was by no means as evil a character as depicted is revealed in the quaint Dialogue of the Chronicle of Azario.

Bernarbò sojourned at Marignano. He hunted in the surrounding woods on horseback, and alone. The day was cold, the hour advanced, and he lost his road. He descried a poor peasant cutting wood.

Bernarbò. The heavens help you, worthy man.

Peasant. I have need of it. In this cold I can do little. The summer was bad; let us hope the winter may be better.

The hunter alighted from his horse. The Dialogue continues thus:

"Friend, you say the summer has been bad. How is that? The harvest has yielded abundantly in grain, and the vintage been good. What has gone wrong?"

Peasant. Oh, we have anew the devil for our master. One hoped that when Signor Bruzio Visconti departed the devil was dead, but we have another master still worse. He takes the bread from our mouths. We poor natives of Lodi work like dogs, and only for his profit.

Bernarbò. Certainly your master does wrong. ... I pray you, friend, guide me out of this wood. It is late; night is near, and I think you, also, have no time to lose, if you seek to return to your own house.

Peasant. Oh, I am in no haste to regain my home. I have left my wife and children in the house with little bread.

Bernarbò. Well, conduct me out of this thicket, and you shall earn something for your trouble.

Peasant. You only seek to turn me from my labour. Perhaps you are an infernal spirit. Cavaliers do not come to this wood. Or, if it please you, pay me first, and I will guide you where you wish.

A World's Shrine

Bernarbò. What do you demand?

Peasant. A *grosso* (three pence) of Milan.

Bernarbò. Once clear of this wood you shall have the *grosso*, and even more.

Peasant. Oh, yes, to-morrow. You are on horseback, and outside the wood you will gallop off, while I remain planted here like a cabbage. Thus do the retainers of our diabolical lord.

Bernarbò. Friend, why will you not believe in my good faith? Here is a pledge.

He gave him the silver buckle of his belt. The *contadino* hid the gift in the bosom of his shirt, and led the way out of the wood, but, very weary, he walked slowly.

Bernarbò. Good man, mount behind me.

Peasant. Do you think your horse can carry two? You are so stout.

Bernarbò. Oh, very well. The horse will carry both of us, and more, especially as, from what you say, you have not dined heavily.

Peasant. You speak the truth.

They traversed the wood.

Bernarbò. Friend, you have given me only

A Sportsman of the Middle Ages

evil tidings of your master. Of the Signor Bernarbò of Milan; what is your opinion of him?

Peasant. They speak well of him. Although he is brutal he maintains order, and if he did not reign even we poor ones would not dare to enter these woods, for fear of assassins, to cut faggots. The Signor Bernarbò maintains justice, and always keeps his word. With the lord of Lodi it is quite different.

The serf complained of one feudal chief who had seized a piece of ground, while others even pillaged household furniture. They escaped from the wood, and, shivering with cold, he alighted, urged Bernarbò to hasten before night, and at the same time wished to restore the buckle, as he would be cast into prison for possessing such a treasure.

Bernarbò. Friend, come with me. I promise you a good inn, a chimney to warm you, and a supper afterwards. To-morrow morning early you can return to your wife.

The peasant hesitated, and then was tempted by the thought of the dozen small loaves the

A World's Shrine

grosso of Milan would purchase to guide the stranger further on his road. They saw torches and bonfires. The lord slyly demanded of his humble companion what the commotion signified. The latter explained that the great Visconti was in the vicinity, fond of hunting alone, and his retainers kindled fires at evening to guide his return. Soon a party came up, and saluted the sportsman respectfully. Bernarbò laughed. The peasant wished himself dead for fright. Bernarbò kept his word. The woodcutter was conducted into a great apartment, warmed before the chimney, and seated at supper with the host. He was then refreshed by a bath, and luxurious bed, and dismissed the next day with further benefits.

Such tales of prince and peasant are as old as kingcraft, but they are especially characteristic of Northern Italy, where the bluff and frank Dukes of Savoy, even to the late King Victor Emmanuel, met such naïve and shrewd rustic opinions of themselves when hunting the chamois in the Alps.

XIII

SPANISH FOOTSTEPS

THE desolation of neglect, isolation, and low-hanging miasma broods over the plain of the Spaniards. The Castle of Fuentes was built by the Governor of Milan in 1603, despite promises to the contrary made to the Grisons by Francesco Sforza. The site, as key to the Valtellina, is emblematic of the sway of these foreign rulers. Colico is near, the Monte Legnone rises beyond, and all about the stronghold the ravages of inundations are discernible, whether of the Maira, and its tributary the Liro, on the side of Chiavenna, or the deposits of the Adda in separating to a narrow channel the Lago di Riva from Como, have wrought their work of depopulation and decay. The Governor of Milan suspected the advantages to the people of a new French treaty for the

A World's Shrine

Grisons and the Valtellina, and erected the castle on the ridge of Montecchio at the entrance to the latter province, to dominate the road to Chiavenna, the lake, and the valley, and thus impede, at will, all trade with the mountain world of Rhetia. The act and motive were eminently Spanish. Francesco Sforza had terminated endless quarrels by a compact not to fortify any post on these routes. Fuentes persisted in his enterprise. He began the work in October, 1603, directed the labours of the military architect Broccardo Borrone of Piacenza on the designs of the engineer Captain Vacallo, and completed it in 1607. He thus closed the commerce with Milan, kept an espionage on intercourse with Venice, and gave rise to the alarm that Spain meditated reconquering the Valtellina. There it stands to this day, sombre, grim, and melancholy, emblem of Spanish rule in other countries; trace of bastion, tower, or chapel discoverable among the shrubs, and tangled grasses of the hillside, with the plain below choked with rushes and marsh waste. The

Spanish Footsteps

Spaniards sought to render the Castle of Fuentes the yoke of the Grisons. In turn the land has designated it as the grave of these conquerors, owing to the slow-sapping fever of the district. King Henry IV. of Navarre is accredited with the opinion that Spain sought here to tie Italy by the throat, and the Grisons by the feet with the same noose. The vipers make of the shell of former greatness their habitation, and the barefooted peasant flees at the warning hiss of the reptiles. Nature is unfriendly to the region in the sluggish overflow of stagnant waters, but the seal of Spain is also apparent in the inertia of past years.

The moralist asserts that the same general traits form the public constitution of men, yet these qualities, modified by individual peculiarities, and taking their course, indicate a virtuous or vicious education, producing crime or nobility, light or darkness. In the same way plants nourish bees and snakes; for one they make honey, and for the other, poison. A corrupt vase sours the mildest liquid. The Plain of the Spaniard long belonged only to the viper and rank weeds, shunned by man.

Pliny's delightful lake region had fallen on evil times in these centuries. The wonder is that one garden terrace was left to bloom, a house not despoiled of all riches, or a church tower left standing amidst the vicissitudes suffered from papal factions and the armies of rival nations sacking and plundering towns and countryside. Many timid natives turned their gaze in the direction of the mountain defiles of Switzerland as a possible refuge from the troubles harassing Italy. The valiant cantons, ever struggling to establish their own independence, were torn by desperate conflicts at the same time. War, pestilence, famine, and floods prevailed in hill and valley; yet Como was renowned for the abundance of her olives, while the Valtellina was known for a delicate cheese, and wax, the fostering of bees serving as an important branch of industry, as well as generous wines which were served at his table by the Abbot of St. Gall to Rudolph of Hapsburg. Also the manufacturing industries of

Spanish Footsteps

.these countries were notable. Coire and Bormio had tariffs of trade with Modena, Como, Venice, and Milan in stuffs, armour, and glass. Fairs were the important marts of intercourse.

The tyranny of the Visconti over Como had begun in dark fashion with Luchino Visconti, and endured in the exactions of Gian Galeazzo. On the death of Filippo Maria Visconti, four pretenders arose: Frederick III., King of the Romans; Alphonse V., of Aragon, heir of the deceased in his testament; Charles, Duke of Orléans, because he was son of Valentina, the daughter of Gian Galeazzo; and Francesco Sforza, as the husband of the illegitimate Bianca. Sforza, as Duke of Milan, harassed Como by reviving ancient taxes and tributes, but hope was not wholly extinguished in the human breast.

Francesco d'Avalos, Marquis of Pescara, held Como in 1521. The little Eden knew what it was to be rifled by French troops and German mercenaries. Other fleets traversed the lake and Lecco, carrying three sail, occasionally, and loaded with bombs. Peace was not permitted to

A World's Shrine

weave her web of prosperity in tranquillity. Como had been perpetually swept by the tempests of conquest and tyranny. Italy, ever the slave of some foreign power since Roman supremacy, was to learn what was the rule of the Spanish taskmaster.

An Italian historian thus laments:

"Wherever Spain has carried her sceptre, desolation and humiliation have resulted. Such was the case in Portugal, in America, in Flanders. Italy learned by the same experience the error of claiming protection of a prince far away, a stranger to all her natural sentiments, as in Charles V., instead of consolidating power under some native ruler acquainted with her needs, and ready to facilitate them. . . . No history leaves in my heart the sadness of the odious Spanish tyranny. Man entirely disappears: in the public laws not the general good, but only ambition, and absurd provision for spying on the populace, exhausting the sources of riches; edicts that speak continually of the need of the king, without considering those of the subject; rapine without ceasing; magistrates, devoid of virtue, shrouding their acts in mystery; monopolies; industry guarded like a thicket; justice sold; the poor cast out in the street; the better classes obliged to establish their own innocence by opening their castles as an asylum for every sort of knavery practised in derision of a weak government and ineffective laws; cities and country overrun by a rabble of soldiery, unpaid from the treasury, and seeking private reimbursement by means of threats and brutality; the shops closed in fear; the land abandoned, uncultivated, because of the enormous taxation. . . . Such has ever been the system."

Charles V. came into an empire more vast than any other since Charlemagne. When he sought Italy he occupied Como and the Castle of Milan. He paid Francesco Sforza an indemnity of nine hundred thousand ducats. Charles was subsequently crowned by the Pope at Bologna. In his rule over Italian affairs he was succeeded by his son Philip II., "a sovereign slow without prudence, ambitious without enterprise, false without ability to deceive, and refined without profundity of subtlety." Philip III. followed. Each monarch showed himself more weak than the other, all betrayed the people, and evinced the despotism, combined with lethargy, which ultimately caused the overthrow of Spain as mistress of the world. Como suffered all the affliction of the rule of these kings, who resembled Midas in the fable and were ever famished in the midst of gold. The governors sent here were charged to extort new taxes, while officials of State instituted a system of insult and depredation on the betrayed people. Colico was once a stretch of twelve thousand acres, planted with mulberry trees, corn, flags, and cane. Made into a county by the Visconti, Charles V. gave it to Sanseverino, Bellaggio to the Sfrondati, the Val Intelvi to Marliani, Lomazzo and Rovellasca to Casnedo, owing to the impecuniosity of the Chamber. P. Giovio pronounced Como, thus despoiled, a city smitten with a moral fever. Lombardy rapidly lost the finer traits of national character, and waxed ignorant, hypocritical, and abject under the Spanish sway. At the same time society became more corrupt, and luxury increased. Como indulged in masquerades, cavalcades with music, poetry, and the erection of triumphal arches in the streets. In 1613 the town boasted of eighteen carriages; in 1672 the

Spanish Footsteps

number had increased to forty-nine. Coaches were inlaid with ebony and ivory, and drawn by four horses. The women were extravagant in costume, and wore long robes of silk and lace. They indulged in perfumes from foreign lands, and disdained native jasmine and rose scents. Spain established the Inquisition, chiefly for the persecution of Jews and witches. A sanctimonious cant was observed. No oil was allowed to be eaten in Lent, and a tax was paid for any animal killed in Como during this season of penance, the sum of money being used for the Duomo.

The most momentous phase of the Spanish supremacy was religious. When Martin Luther lifted his voice against the sale of indulgences by Pope Leo in 1517, Como and the region turned a page, also, in the history of the Reformation. In vain Charles V. convoked the Diet of Worms in 1512, to check the progress of the Lutheran doctrines, and involved Germany in war and tribulation. All the world, aghast, was required to contemplate the defiance of a new order that sought to found such dogmas as the overthrow of papal authority, refusal to admit celibacy for the priesthood, baptism, the holy supper, the saints, purgatory, the confessional, — in fact, allegiance to Rome.

There is a popular tradition that Martin Luther preached in many places around the Lake of Como, and was driven from the pulpit at Menaggio. Calvin is believed to have visited the court of Ferrara in 1535, disguised, to see the Duchess Rénée of France. Contemporaneously with Luther, the curate Ulric Zwingli preached the same doctrines at Zurich. In the agitations, tumults, and bitter persecutions that ensued, fugitives fled from all countries to Switzerland.

Voltaire has affirmed that few Italians gave their adherence to the Lutheran doctrines, as a people too much occupied with pleasure and intrigue to take part in the serious disturbances of the time. Arnold of Brescia preached at Zurich in the twelfth century. Such Italians are cited as Giorgio Francispergio, a fanatical apostle of Lutheranism, who carried in his pocket a golden cord with which to strangle Clement VII. as the

Spanish Footsteps

last of the Popes, and passed by the Lake of Como in the day of the Medicean wars, and paused at Sorico, where he deposited a colossal head of Pompey, taken in the famous sack of Rome. He went to Paris. Francesco Calvo of Menaggio was an ardent reformer, praised by Erasmus of Rotterdam, and made known to Luther for his erudition. He distributed the writings of Luther, printed at Bâle, through the Alps. Many illustrious women were suspected of cherishing the new opinions, the Duchess of Urbino, Julia, Gonzaga, Countess of Fondi, and even Vittoria Colonna.

Beyond that northern gate of Como rose the Valtellina and the Grisons. The Valtellina was a fine and important province, called fertile at as remote a period as when Cassiodorus wrote in praise of Como, and coveted, ever, by Milan, rival Bishops, and Como. The Grisons formed an Etruscan relic in the Alps. The people were poor and independent in spirit, building their huts among inaccessible rocks. They were menaced by the Romans, and then by all

A World's Shrine

Europe. The feudal lords, and the bishops built castles in the land. This mountain realm became one of the chosen asylums of men who desired to praise God in their own fashion. Is there not an element of the cool air, the scent of the pines skirting the ledges, and the icy pinnacles of glacier and peak in the thought? Carlyle truly said: "No iron chain, or outward force of any kind, can ever compel the soul of man to believe, or disbelieve."

A Protestant is still known in the Grisons as a *Lutero*. The Bible was translated by G. Diodati. The Confession of Faith, signed at Coire, April, 1553, admitted the three Symbols, the Paternoster, the Decalogue, the observance of Sunday, the two sacraments of baptism and the communion. Such was the code of the pastors of Rhetia.

At the close of the nineteenth century man is not imprisoned, tortured, or executed for religion. He worships or discredits according to his own moral convictions. Surely there is a profound interest, quite apart from creeds, even in a casual

Spanish Footsteps

glance at those of an earlier time who suffered, fought, and struggled in spiritual conflict, from Rudolph de Salis of Solio, whose tomb records that he was driven from his home by human machinations, but returned, and died free, to Vergerio, the Papal Nuncio in Germany, who fled to the Valtellina, humiliated, impoverished, and accused of heresy.

Yonder is the Plain of the Spaniard, with trace of the Castle of Fuentes on the ridge, favourite haunt of the viper. Joseph II. abolished the fort, and Colonel Schreder, the last castellan, cultivated mulberry trees around it. The French, with five hundred soldiers, in command of General Rambaud, in 1796 mined, and blew it up. A solid portion of masonry resisted destruction. Spanish footsteps! All national interests stagnated in the administration of the government monopolies, and taxes. Manufactories and commerce languished. In Italy work and enterprise, artistic, agricultural, and trade had been promoted by princes and ecclesiastics, in various channels, but the Spanish rule exacted a noble

A World's Shrine

indolence. All occupation was derogatory to a count or a marquis. The town duties checked industry. As a result, the artisans of Como migrated to Venice and foreign lands in large numbers, just as the Protestants of Locarno sought Switzerland, when the brave little land opened the door of Uri, Schwyz, Lucerne, Zug, Unterwald, Soleure, and Fribourg to such exiles. Prosperity was curbed in the valleys of Chiasso, Gandino, and Mendrisio in a similar mode. Como lamented the reduction of her commerce for weavers, dyers, workers in iron and glass and woollen fabrics by more than half. The Valtellina had a proverb that all riches were dissipated in five ways: one portion went to the princes, one to the ecclesiastics, one to the nobility, one to agricultural failure, and one to the waters.

"History is little more than the register of the crimes, follies, and misfortunes of mankind," said Gibbon.

Pian di Spagna! Low-trailing mists of heat over stagnant waters, sedgy wastes, and desertion!

Spanish Footsteps

The whole history of Spain, as a foreign ruler, is embodied in this dreary picture. Alecto shook from her locks her favourite snake to seek the wakeful Amata, glide near, seize her cooler senses by degrees, in silent insidious venom, and sting her to the heart. Alecto was Spain, and Amata, Italy.

The Englishman of the last century is still quoted who marvelled that Richelieu expended so many soldiers, and so much money to prevent Spain from holding such a little country as the Valtellina. Lord Chesterfield pronounced the traveller a triple idiot not to understand that the province furnished the only road to Austria and the Tyrol for Spain.

XIV

A WITCH

YOU half believe that she is really a witch as you step on shore from the boat and first perceive her seated at the door of her house twisting her distaff. No doubt she rides over the lake on a broomstick at midnight. She is clad in rags of a sombre tint, and has some sort of drapery — shawl or kerchief — gathered over her head. Her features are yellow and wrinkled, the glance of her eye covert and distrustful, her smile malicious and sinister. Craven and superstitious humanity may prefer to bid her good-morrow with civility rather than arouse her ire by careless rudeness, and have her practising dread incantations behind one's back, with the sticking of pins into a wax doll or a sheep's head — a favourite pastime of hags in all countries, apparently. She is

A Witch

akin to the crones of the world, a class curiously devoid of nationality and country. She might be found as readily on an Alpine crag, in the woods of Germany or Scandinavia, Great Britain and America, as on the Mediterranean shores, in the darkest, most tortuous Venetian Calle, and Como. In type she is ever the same. She is a fascinating terror to the youthful mind as a bogy of nursery admonitions, and a mysterious tool of evil for the unscrupulous of mankind. Magical plants spring up about her footsteps: nightshade, hellebore, the golden blossom that reveals the spot where treasure is buried, the flower of the pine to avert bad dreams. She gathers fungus of strange growth, and does a little trade in amulets and philtres destined to influence the career of the wearer. Her pets are usually uncanny of aspect, in the way of black cats, owlets, and crippled falcons, readily converted by the lively imagination into familiar spirits. Are there not still elder-tree witches, with the hare-bell and foxglove especially dedicated to the crew, in addition? The mountain ash averts

A World's Shrine

lightning, as the first hazel twig cut in the spring saves the grain in storms.

Witchcraft is very ancient. If the Chinese tie a red ribbon around the wrist of a child to ward off such evil spirits, the Highlanders adopt a similar strip for the tails of their cows. There were witches in the time of the Plinys, possibly allied in classical days with the astrologers and soothsayers. Pliny the Younger, Cato, Livy, and Tacitus laughed at them and the superstitions attached to their magical powers, as well as at the ladies and gentlemen who gave credence to the interpretation of dreams and portents by these oracles. Especial heed was early accorded to the devil as a power, combined with a dread of haunted houses and credence in phantoms. In the Valtellina credit is reputed to be still given to rich misers, after death, seeking the Val di Togno to dig with a pickaxe and cast down stones. All through the land there are fields of the witches, as in the Valley of Sementina, near Bellinzona, and in the vicinity of Como. Certain lonely huts and dismantled ruins near Lugano,

A Witch

Locarno, and in the Valtellina are known for witches' houses, as they were in the day of Pliny. The Roman and Lombard laws sought to suppress the folly. The populace inclined to tales of the marvellous. Wild and foolish rumours may have always been current of the powers of wizard folk. This one could cast spells, inspired by love or hate, on man, animals, and the flowering crops. That one could convert a piece of wood into a horse, an ass, a goat, at pleasure. They made ointments of rare efficacy, powders of enchantment, and charms. The chances are these boasters wished the palm crossed, gypsy fashion, to avert such malign deeds.

The witch of Como may well be accorded a special place in history. Her native hamlet of Lezzeno rests in shadow, set deep under the wood of San Primo. The sun does not visit the locality during the winter. All about the spot are rocky ravines and cascades, with Torno to the south. The houses are roofed with crumbled tiles, the walls are painted white and yellow, with blue facings here and there, and connected by slimy passages or vaulted archway. The inhabitants of these shady and forbidding haunts seem to have early acquired a dark reputation for dealing in witchcraft and magic above their fellows.

Is the crone a lineal descendant of the witch of Theocritus, or the Libyan sorceress of Virgil, versed in supernatural lore? Does a wild and even poetical interest attach to her of orgies similar to the Walpurgis Night on the Blocksberg, or gatherings around the tree of Benevento? Neighbours born on a Friday of March may consider themselves lucky as thereby placed beyond her power. Who knows how many fine ladies consult her in their love affairs, and seek some more subtle draught of fresh bewitchment wherewith to ensnare cavaliers than their own beauty?

In the fifteenth and sixteenth centuries these old women's fables had a phase of tragedy. Spain sought to exterminate heresy and Black Art in all her possessions. The Inquisition was organised at Como with reference to witchcraft as well. Morbid imagination ran riot. The arrows

A Village Street

A Witch

of suspicion and detection flew far and wide. Poor old women were not the only victims, but all classes were struck, by means of bribery, terror, and the seizing of property of those deemed guilty, as well as the despoiling of the heirs of prisoners. The confessions made to the Inquisition condemned the wretched culprits, and implicated others, according to the authorities at Chiavenna, Berbenno, or Mendrisio. The most painful absurdities were related of the condemned, of intercourse with the Evil One, transformations, and conversations with Diana and Herodias. (Why were these ladies introduced into such society?) The fantasies of the popular taste seemed to demand marvels.

Fra Bernardo Rategno of Como, the zealous Inquisitor of 1505, wrote a book entitled "De Strigiis." He stated that the witches met the devil, in human form, on the nights before Friday to render him homage and express disrespect for the Cross, the Madonna, the Confessional. "How to discover the witches?" demanded Rategno.

A World's Shrine

St. Dominic burned heretics. A bull of Pope Pius II., dated March, 1493, accused the people of Rezzonico of sorcery. The bishops visited the surrounding villages in consequence, interrogated the parishioners, and detected many witches and magicians among them. The Bishop Filippo Visconti then had them exorcised. Also Piero Antonio Stampa of Chiavenna, curate of Delebio, published the *Fuga dæmonum*. Five persons were burned at Como, and three at Lugano. A woman was broken on the wheel in 1519, on the accusation of having killed men, women, and children with the unpleasant aim of eating them. Hebrews were executed on slight pretext. Sixtus V. issued a bull, in 1585, condemning all witches.

From Pope to Puritan was but a step in the excitement of a popular madness infecting many lands. Who maketh us to differ in human wisdom? The descendant of a New England judge is aware that he condemned several innocent women as witches, with firmest conviction in his own prejudice of so-called duty as a religious

A Witch

citizen, — a crime which he strove to expiate, in later years, by fasting and prayer. What was the original source of the witchcraft persecution? The wicked smote the innocent, and the pious carried out their will, aided by the tumults of the crowd. The Jews have suffered expulsion, been accused of fearful deeds, and despoiled of their possessions as the actual motive. The suppression of the order of the Knights Templar, on the plea of mysterious idolatry worship, seems to have been to seize their property. Who knows if the witches of England and America, as well as under the espionage of the Inquisition, possessed riches coveted by their neighbours, and the unjust extortion of the inheritance of the widow and orphan, or the old lady of rank, had much to do with the burning at the stake, and subsequent confiscation of goods?

The witch of Lezzeno need fear no such fate under modern government. She sits at her door twirling the distaff through the long summer day. A group of young women are washing their household linen down on the brink of the water.

A World's Shrine

Their voices and laughter rise, from time to time, mingled with the song of birds. A matron toils up the path with one of the creel-baskets of the country on her back, containing a variety of articles, such as a bag of meal, an earthenware pot, a bundle of clover and grass, a wooden bowl and ladle. She exchanges polite greetings, and rests her burden on the ledge of wall, planting her brown, well-shaped bare feet on the ground.

"How fares it with you, Carlotta?" inquires the witch.

"Eh! The flour of the devil goes all to bran," replies Carlotta, wearily.

"*Pazienza!* You have your boys. Three cords make a rope. I am alone."

Poor body! Perhaps she is not a witch after all, and no more addicted to broomstick-riding at midnight than you or I, gentle reader.

XV

THE MAGICIANS

THE whole world belongs to the magicians, and they, in return, are the world's servants. Earth and the atmosphere perpetually yield them precious secrets, yet they seek more. Inspired by an insatiable curiosity, they peer into the unfathomed mysteries of the universe, and are now baffled, and again enlightened by the luminous intuitions of their own intellect. Of all men the magicians are fashioned in the image of God, for their powers are Godlike. At least their Creator has sent them forth as his messengers to interpret matters hidden to average humanity. To-day they solidify the air into a block by means of the newly discovered element argon. What will they achieve to-morrow?

A World's Shrine

One of the number crossed the seas, recently, and paused on the shores of Como. All his senses, held in acute tension of study, were cradled by the soothing repose of the nook. Fame was his of modern celebrity, but he wore his laurels lightly, and with modesty. He was christened by his generation a Paracelsus, and in the development of pure magic the Wizard of the West. Waking or sleeping he beheld ever new realms to conquer, for there is no finality to science. A marvellous personality was his own. Now he evolved some epoch-making problem to help mankind forward, in his laboratory and now he dallied, in childish mood, with a fairyland of toys, the whispering box to imprison and give back the notes of songs, and words. His whims possessed a certain fascination to the public in their originality. He was as prone to consider the labour-saving broom in "the household of Research," a humble Cinderella in the manipulation of trifles, as to adhere to the realm of purely theoretical philosophy, and the wielding of mighty power to move machinery.

The Magicians

Como has weather as capricious as the native temperament, all smiles, frowns, and tears.

Thus, as the magician paused on a terrace overlooking the lake, the sunshine suddenly paled, and the atmosphere grew sultry. With an incredible rapidity of transition from tranquillity, a wan, grey pallor touched the surface of the water and the sky, while a purple gloom deepened over the mountains, and filled the ravines. Timid folk hid themselves in the depths of chambers with closed shutters, and nervous menials dropped trays, loaded with bottles, glass, and porcelain, causing a resounding clamour. The wind moaned fitfully, almost palpable darkness descended, and the awful crash of thunder burst on the startled, cowering Paradise, succeeded by lightning in sheets of fire, forked chains athwart the gloom, and hissing serpent tongues. Hail roughened the wavelets to mimic billows, and whipped the sprays of flowers mercilessly of colour and form. Rain in torrents devastated the hillside and vineyards in widespread ruin for the husbandman.

A World's Shrine

The Lake district has kept a dolorous record in the annals of centuries of similar disasters, when the thunderbolt smote rocks to their foundations, and lightning shattered venerable trees to the core. In an hour the sky might be again blue, the sun bright, and the mountain tops powdered with freshly fallen snow. Volta witnessed and noted the result of such a tempest in 1822.

The magician looked on with calm front, and folded arms. He discerned luminiferous ether in the play of the lightning, a conducting medium following the lines of force on all sides, a substance filling space, and drawn from the twilight of Nature's penetralia. This lightning of Como seemed to possess a particular significance to the visitor. He was prepared for every caprice and mockery of which the element is capable. Truly electricity moves more rapidly than light or sound; eye and ear may be paralysed before light and sound can make an impression on them. What course would this primary spirit, malicious, *bizarre* in pranks, clairvoyant or blind as to

The Magicians

result, voluntary and mysterious, follow on Como? It might shatter a church tower and fall on a group of the faithful gathered on the pavement below; twist the prongs of the pitchfork into a corkscrew shape, carried on the shoulder of a peasant; stamp the photograph of an adjacent pine-tree on the flesh of the lad killed bird-nesting in the poplar; carbonise one man without trace of violence to his surroundings, and rend off the clothing of another leaving him unscathed.

"Tell me what electricity is, and I will tell you all the rest," mused the magician, in the words of Lord Kelvin.

He entered the skiff of Memory, and traversed the lake, borne by the swift current, without need of sail or rudder. He sought the tomb of Volta at the Villa di Campora.

Alessandro Volta was born at Como in 1745. He belonged to an ancient family. Of four brothers, a Dominican, an archdeacon, and a canon, his father had entered upon the career of a Jesuit, when, after eleven years of seclusion, he returned to the world, and married Maddalena of the

A World's Shrine

noble house of Inzaghi. He founded a new family, of three daughters and four sons. Two brothers became canons of the Duomo, one a Dominican, and the fourth the famous scholar Alessandro. Early deprived of paternal care, the latter was left in charge of his uncle, the archdeacon. He was destined for the law. Volta was another example of the boy of genius intended by a domestic authority for a career wholly at variance with a natural bent of instinct. Voltaire held that all artists who have attained great renown cultivated their powers in opposition to their parents, and because nature was stronger than education. Molière, the young Poquelin, was expected to follow his father's trade of upholsterer, while paternal wisdom ordained that Michelangelo should be a wool-comber, Correggio a butcher, Andrea del Sarto, a tailor, Guido Reni, a musician, and Salvator Rosa a priest.

Volta was sent to school, and seems to have early developed a lively and insubordinate intelligence. He had curiosity to fathom natural phenomena, and readily surpassed his fellow-

The Magicians

pupils in devouring all the works on philosophy within his reach. A peasant described a spring at Monteverde to the boy, where bits of sparkling gold had been seen. Volta is said to have hastened to the spot, and nearly drowned himself in clutching the yellow mica which had deceived the country folk. He wrote poems in Latin. One of eight hundred lines was descriptive of the seasons. Another little poem still more betrayed his inclinations, as it treated of metals, gunpowder, *ignis-fatuus*, and electricity. He was placed in a Jesuit seminary. In vain these new preceptors strove to curb his spirit, and even forbade him to work on favourite pursuits as misspent time, in a testy, conventional, school-master fashion. The youthful aspirant to fame is reputed to have retorted in a defiant, not to say disrespectful manner. The worthy fathers thereupon prophesied he would come to no good end. He pursued his own course, meditating on physics with such enlightenment as the day afforded. He experimented with ribbons, rosin, pieces of sulphur, and thin staves of wood soaked in oil, groping ever to seize an idea of maintaining electric currents. Benjamin Franklin was already described by his contemporaries as a Jupiter who had grasped the thunderbolts of heaven. Le Monnier discovered that the air is always electric. In 1769 Volta wrote a treatise "On the Attractive Force of Electric Fire," and in 1775 invented an electrophorus. He became a professor of Natural Philosophy at Pavia, and retained the post for thirty years. His celebrity rests on the discovery of the voltaic pile, an apparatus which excites a continuous current of electricity by contact with different substances. Sir John Herschel pronounced it the most wonderful of human adaptations in the minute and delicate effects obtained through the medium of a series of well conducted, and logically combined experiments. Volta visited Tuscany in 1774, and was received with great honours. Later he met Franklin, de Saussure, Chaptal, Vauquelin, Laplace, De Luc, Banks, Vaumarum, Gilberte, and the Emperor Joseph II. He received the Copley gold medal at London. In Paris he experimented with his pile before the Institute, and was made one of the eight foreign associates in 1802. Beauharnais attached the Legion of Honour to his breast, while Bonaparte created him a Count of the Italian order. He married a lady of his native town, Teresa Pellegrini, and had three sons. Most suggestive is the fact that Alexander I. invited the savant to Russia; but he preferred to remain under the sky of Como. He died in March, 1827, at the age of eighty-two years.

According to Bacon, all the sciences are branches of one trunk. We find in the rectification of certain errors in the theory of Galvani, made by Volta, the frog of fame, and a little kindred crew of the first tiny martyrs to science in vivisection. The frog naturally takes precedence as having hopped — or flopped — into the front rank of an unenviable celebrity, from a batrachian point of view. Was not this renowned frog made to contribute its hind legs, as a delicacy, to the invalid broth of Madame Galvani of Bologna, whether it would or no? Did not a consequent squirming of its members arouse a general inter-

A World's Shrine

est of wise heads, if the lady's appetite was not impaired? In due time the mouse, the lizard, and the sparrow were subjected to dissection in search of animal magnetism and electricity. If the modern magician, dealing to-day with the labours of Helmholtz and Kirchhoff, and the electric waves of Heinrich Hertz, pays homage to the tomb of Volta at the Villa di Campora, not only the shade of the savant welcomes him. Surely the spectres of a doleful little procession cross his path, and regard him mournfully with wee, beady eyes, — the frog of Galvani, the mouse of the laboratory, the dejected lizard, and the crestfallen, erewhile saucy, sparrow. These seem to pipe, in the name of the whole animal kingdom: "Oh, big and enlightened mortal, how would you like it yourself to have your nerve tissues photographed and your spinal marrow searchingly investigated?"

Electric globes shine softly on the town of Como at night. They are the glowing memory of her great son Alessandro Volta. The Centenary Exhibition of 1899 was a fresh tribute to

The Magicians

the early genius, from collections of primitive batteries, quaintly suggestive of the past, intricate machinery for designing embroideries and silk, lithographic printing, metal work, and the moving of looms by electricity, to the development of locomotion in vehicles and boats on the waters. The hand of the magicians still grasps the magic sceptre.

XVI

"ALL THE WORLD'S A STAGE"

IF Como reminds the visitor of the theatre, no place on the shore is as much like artificial scenery as the Villa d'Este, with its wide marble façade and portico, gardens extending up the hillside, groves of pine and cypress, and terrace steps leading to the water, with pleasure boats moored beneath the boundary wall.

Verily the paint-pots of the stage carpenter and the scenic artist have no cobalt, madder, or burnt umber of deeper tints than the ripples washing the terrace brink and the parterres and flower beds on all sides. One may not be especially attracted to the stately mansion shut in under the hills, any more than deeply sympathetic with the heroine of the spot, yet there is a cer-

HOME OF QUEEN CAROLINE

tain mirage of beauty and unreality in the somnolent hours, heavy with the scents of exotics, spent here.

The knight Lohengrin, clad in shimmering armour, should advance to embark in the swan-boat in lieu of the brisk traveller, with a red guide-book in his hand, just alighted from an omnibus at the *Hôtel de la Reine d'Angleterre*. The modern Juliet in a lace tea-gown, who emerges on a balcony to warn Romeo, seated in a garden-chair below, with an illustrated journal, that the kettle is boiling, should muse, instead, on the advisability of cutting up the young gentleman into little stars and set in the firmament of her devotion.

The Villa d'Este was the residence of Caroline of Brunswick for five years. The property originally belonged to Cardinal Gallio.

A drama is here performed in five acts for the edification of the casual observer. The leading actress is the Princess of Wales, and the audience posterity.

When the curtain rises the scene presents a

A World's Shrine

perspective of gardens stretching up the slope, with fountains, arbours, grottoes of shell-work, and statues placed on pedestals amidst dark shrubbery. Princess Caroline appears in the distance, and slowly descends the main path, pausing to pluck a real flower here and there. (One would expect her nosegay to be made of muslin and tinsel, even on Como, under the circumstances.) The poor lady was considered pretty in early youth, with blond hair, and fine features, but now her figure has become ball-like, and her head appears too large for throat and shoulders. At the sight of hearers, however listless and indifferent to her woes this *fin de siècle* audience may be, she bewails her lot, and takes all into her confidence without too much tact of discretion in the desire to arouse sympathy. Alas! The world is selfish, hard, and, as a rule, not at all interested in unhappy heroines, whose mood varies from tears to assumed jocularity and satire over the wounding slights of enemies. The Princess Caroline tells the public all about it in her broken English, and Frenchified German.

"All the World's a Stage"

Listen! She, Caroline Amelia Elisabeth, daughter of the Duke of Brunswick, left her father's court on December thirtieth, 1794, attended by her mother and a brilliant retinue, to marry Prince George of Wales. She was about to make a great match. King George III., her uncle, had selected her as bride, while Queen Charlotte preferred the beautiful and accomplished Louisa, Princess of Mecklenburg, afterwards Queen of Prussia. She rested at Hanover, embarked at Cuxhaven on board the "Jupiter" in March, 1795, dropped anchor at the Nore, reached Gravesend in a fog, and disembarked at Greenwich. Here Princess Caroline steps to the wing of the tiny stage of Villa d' Este, and the scenes shift slowly before the spectator to London in the background, panorama-wise. She smiles across the footlights, and indicates the triumphs of her entry on wedded life. Behold London at the dawn of the nineteenth century. The bride is driven in the king's coach, with six horses, and escorted by the Prince's Regiment of Light Dragoons, commanded by Lord Edward Somer-

A World's Shrine

set. The equipage crosses Westminster Bridge, the mighty sea of populace thronging the avenues of park and palace. The crowd cheers, and the bride smiles and bows.

The scene changes to the interior of St. James Palace. The betrothed couple dine together at five o'clock, and make each other's acquaintance. According to respectful chroniclers Prince George is handsome, accomplished, of polished and graceful address, versed in ancient languages, conversant with French, German, and Italian, music, and belles lettres. In fact he is "the happiest mixture of conscious dignity and unaffected affability." After dinner a distinguished group of actors file in: King George III., kindly encouraging to his new daughter-in-law, Queen Charlotte coolly critical in bearing, the royal princesses under their august mother's supervision, Prince William, and the Dukes of Clarence and Gloucester. Her Serene Highness approaches the embrasure, and makes her little speech in English to the people gathered before the palace:

"Believe me I am very happy and delighted

"All the World's a Stage"

to see the good and brave English people — the best nation upon earth."

Is not all this very stagey? The going out on the balcony of sovereigns to salute their subjects always smacks of the theatre and the appearance of the leading actors before the drop-curtain.

The scene is replaced by another of St. James Chapel, where the Archbishop of Canterbury waits to perform the marriage ceremony. The pageant is of the richest, comprising all the corps of the theatre, and nearly of a nation. The procession wends across the stage in interminable length of state officials, peers, and dignitaries in sumptuous robes. Trumpeters and a master of ceremonies precede the bride, in her regal coronet, led by the Duke of Clarence, and her train borne by four daughters of earls. Next appear heralds, officers, the lord chamberlain, and the prince, wearing the collar of the Garter, and escorted by the dukes of Bedford and Roxburgh. The suite of Their Majesties follow. Knights, archbishops, households, the sword of state, borne in pomp, surround the monarch. The queen ad-

A World's Shrine

vances in turn, accompanied by princesses of the blood and ladies. The theatrical wardrobe is rifled of velvet, ermine, jewels, gold lace, and satin for the occasion. Cannon boom out from park and tower, bells ring, and London is illuminated with myriads of tapers arranged in shapes and designs that night in honour of the auspicious occasion.

The curtain falls on this first act, leaving Princess Caroline to her reminiscences. The audience, posterity, smiles superciliously at the idea of town-lighting before the day of gas and electricity.

The second act finds the exile in a sad humour. She is seated before her *escritoire* dabbling in that most mischievous of all feminine gifts, letter-writing. Like many other women, Princess Caroline wrote too many letters. These light leaflets of jest, complaint, satire, justification, and confidence scattered broadcast from her pen brought her a crop of dragon's teeth in the sowing. The queen was scandalised at the frankness of her stated opinions of those about her, and the cour-

"All the World's a Stage"

tiers followed the royal example in seeking a pretext of disapproval. Never was bride surrounded by a greater number of enemies at the outset. Lady Jersey, watching in the background, was alert to inform the prince that Caroline had incautiously gossiped of certain German suitors for her hand. The prince sneered readily at his consort. The barbed arrow was launched at the breast of the bride that he only married at all in order to have his debts paid. She is of a high descent and a haughty spirit. The bitter cup of neglect, humiliation, and a return to earlier favourites was held to her lips. The king maintained his attitude of consideration for his unfortunate niece. The queen and the princesses scarcely visited her. The courtiers ebbed away, swept by the " besom of expediency." Princess Caroline, in her difficult rôle, needed to possess the patience of a Griselda and the wisdom of Solomon. She had neither qualification in marked degree. She belonged to the eccentric House of Brunswick.

She lays aside her pen, rises, and confronts the public, philosophising thus:

A World's Shrine

"Suspense is very great bore, but we live only de poor beings of de hour, and we ought always to try to make us happy so long we do live. To tell you God's truth, I have had as many vexations as most people, but we must make up *vous* mind to enjoy de good spite of de bad, and I mind, now, de last no more dan dat."

She snaps her fingers contemptuously.

The curtain sweeps down on the second act. The audience, posterity, yawns behind its fan, and is manifestly bored by the dreary monologue.

When the little stage is once more visible no less a person than "the first gentleman in Europe" steps forward, jauntily, with an eye, not on such beauty as may be present, as much as the effect produced on the spectators by himself. He poses marvellously well, and the rouge on his cheeks is artistically adjusted. Domestic affairs may jar, and the mob, with primitive ideas of conjugal duty, be hostile to him as the heir. He has just written an address to the king. He gives a brief extract: —

"All the World's a Stage"

"I ask to be allowed to display the best energies of my character, to shed the last drop of my blood in support of Your Majesty's person, crown, and dignity; for this is not a war for empire, glory, or dominion, but for existence [1803]. In this contest the lowest and humblest of Your Majesty's subjects have been called on; it would little become me, who am the first, and who stand at the very footstool of the throne, to remain a tame, an idle, and a lifeless spectator of the mischiefs which threaten us, unconscious of the dangers surrounding us, and indifferent to the consequences. Hanover is lost; England is threatened with invasion; Ireland is in rebellion; Europe is at the foot of France. At such a moment the Prince of Wales, yielding to none of your servants in zeal and devotion, to none of your subjects in duty, none of your children in tenderness and affection, presumes to approach you to repeat offers of services already made."

The actor toys with the paper complacently. What does the audience think of it? Are not the periods rather neatly turned? Posterity is amazed, even electrified. Can this stately gentleman, inspired by such noble sentiments, be the

A World's Shrine

lord of Princess Caroline, the father of young Charlotte, the comrade of the Earl of Moira, and Admiral Jack Bayne, who keeps his bed until three or four o'clock of an afternoon, and otherwise sets at defiance the laws of health?

The heir makes his bow, and quits the boards, to become prince regent, in due course of time, with the old king stricken mad.

Act fourth portrays Princess Caroline in melancholy plight. She holds the scene, and describes, with volubility, her wrongs to all listeners. A separation had long been in contemplation between the royal pair. The prince lived at Windsor and Carlton House. She had retired to Charlton near Blackheath, with her daughter the Princess Charlotte, and ladies-in-waiting. With the insanity of George III. she must lose her only partisan. Her child was taken from her for suitable education. Tears and sobs check the utterance of the mother at this juncture. The poor lady may not be a great actress, but she rises to a climax of tragedy. She is, for the moment, a Niobe, full of dignity and grandeur

"All the World's a Stage"

before the world. The prince regent found his consort an unfit guardian for Charlotte. He wished her to live with him. The affront to maternal dignity had a double sting. She was an unsuitable guardian of the heiress to the throne. Still less was he a paternal example to youth. The regent had further expressed a desire to never meet his wife again, in public or private. In 1806 reports injurious to the character of the lady were circulated. The chronicler hastened to add, "in order to intimidate her." Ah! Princess Caroline may well exclaim with Timon:

> "I am sick of this false world, and will love nought
> But even the bare necessities upon 't."

She retires overwhelmed by chagrin and sorrow. Her daughter had been presented at Court, and she not admitted to the Drawing-room.

Then Princess Charlotte trips on the stage for a brief moment. She is a blooming maiden of eighteen years, endowed with plenty of character. There is a trait of frankness and honesty in her adherence to her mother. Has not the populace

A World's Shrine

admonished her to stand up for the injured parent? She pouts at her father, defies her grandmother, Queen Charlotte, and openly rebels at her governesses. She runs away in a hackney coach to pay her mother a visit at Connaught House. Princess Caroline is absent at Blackheath. Young Charlotte throws herself down petulantly on a couch, and affirms:

"I would rather earn my own bread, and live on five shillings a week, than lead the life I do."

Then the Archbishop of Canterbury comes to fetch the naughty girl home before her mother's return. She hangs her head, and goes, to become a young lady, with a marriage to the Prince of Orange in contemplation, and the ultimate choice of Leopold of Saxe-Coburg. Defeated, and fearing imprisonment, in some form, Princess Caroline leaves England for the Continent.

The audience, posterity, sighs, is moved, ill-at-ease, hopes it will soon finish. It must have all happened so long ago!

In the final act Princess Caroline strolls about the gardens of Villa d'Este. She is attired in a

"All the World's a Stage"

white robe, and wears on her head a cap of crêpe with lavender bows. This costume is mourning for her daughter, Princess Charlotte, whose early death surprised the nation. Princess Caroline is weary, disillusioned with the paradise where she has planted flowers and built roads, after the example of such an enterprising lady as Napoleon's sister, Elisa Bonaparte, Queen of Etruria, and restless. The exile has dwelt at Naples, Genoa, and Pesaro. She has mingled with the cosmopolitan society of the Italy of that day. She values it little, and wishes that she had never abandoned her position in England. She advances down the stage. A despatch is presented to her by an attendant. The year 1820 has dawned and George IV. will be crowned king. She raises her head, and pauses at the footlights. She will return to England, and claim her right of being proclaimed queen. She bids adieu to Villa d'Este for ever!

The audience, posterity, disperses slowly, pondering on the sequel to this strange drama, of how the king had the name of his consort struck from

A World's Shrine

the liturgy. A supreme moment of vindication came for Queen Caroline. She arrived at Canterbury, and her journey to London was a triumphal one. The populace rallied in her support, mobs threatened, flags were hoisted, and seditious placards posted. She appeared undaunted before the House of Lords during the preparation of the bill of separation. The coronation took place in July, 1821. The queen appeared at the entrance of Westminster Abbey, and was refused admittance. The repulse hastened her end. She died in August, and her remains were taken to Brunswick at her own request.

The audience, posterity, contemplates these problems of history. If the nose of Cleopatra had been less symmetrical the face of the earth would have been materially modified. If an inflammatory fever had not seized Mirabeau, a tile had fallen on Robespierre, or a bullet struck Bonaparte, events would have had different results. If Louisa of Mecklenburg had married George IV. how would the German Empire have

"All the World's a Stage"

been shaped by Bismarck for that fine old gentleman Kaiser Wilhelm to rule over? If Queen Caroline had been more tractable, as wife and mother, the fairies would have watched in vain around the cradle in 1819, of Victoria Alexandrina, daughter of the Duke of Kent, for the Victorian era.

The curtain falls at Villa d'Este, the lights burn dim, and the play, called Life, is over for Caroline of Brunswick to all eternity.

XVII

A MUSICAL MEMORY

THE tall and slender form of a priest, in a black robe, paced the path bordered by orange and citron trees. The seminarist had come from Rome, and his sphere of cloistered studies, at the invitation of the proprietor long absent in foreign lands. Something notable would be expected of him in his day, perhaps. His soul of the musician was full of half-awakened harmonies. His education had taken him back to the date when music lay yet in the cradle, awaiting the touch of Italy upon her strings, the touch of Germany upon her keys. The Gregorian Chaunts, the themes of Pergolesi, and even the graceful imagination of Metastasio had long absorbed him.

A Musical Memory

With Schleiermacher he believed that religion is a music, pervading all our sentiments, thoughts, and acts.

Hedges of bay and ilex framed a belvedere, and a tiny amphitheatre of lawn, with an obelisk rising in the centre. On all sides of the boundary the property was embowered in laurel. The visitor might find here a sunny garden, a cool banquet-hall, and watch the play of the central fountain, with antique bronze reliefs, where the spray blown by zephyrs rose in a silvery veil, aspired to the heights, swayed, and lapsed back earthward to repose once more. How many have enjoyed this courteous hospitality of generations of patrician owners.

To the seminarist the place was peopled with ghosts; a shadowy company of sweetest suggestiveness to his own meditations and aspirations. All were friendly, and all smiled on him. The brotherhood had attained immortality, crossed the boundary chasm between life and death, climbed to new realms of harmony. Did not Beethoven, colossal and profound in thought,

A World's Shrine

Mozart, melancholy yet majestic, and Mendelssohn, full of power and technical skill, or Wagner, among the clouds of the great ideal, beckon to him to struggle forward in a daring boldness of conception of the fugue movement, or, at least, to attain sincerity and truthfulness in his work? Alas! would he ever presume to write a symphony after Beethoven's Ninth, which Wagner designated as the last possible emanation of music as a separate art? Could he hope to follow Mozart's Jupiter symphony, or charm the ear of his generation by even an echo of Mendelssohn's elves and fairies? Still nearer to him the composers of the sonata, the fantasia, the song, linking together words and melody, of his own day, brushed him by an impalpable presence, wafted to him, in the fountain's spray, as he passed in his walk, in all the manifold phases of a subtle language speaking to the human heart; Schubert's rich lyrics, Schumann, first of subjective romanticists, and Brahms, with his store of chamber music. The seminarist folded his arms across his breast, and watched the upward puls-

A Musical Memory

ing of the water jet, absorbed in reverie. Should he be a great tone-poet also, capable of maintaining the fixed relations of separate parts of some composition on consecrated themes, the resurrection, the sorrows of Mary; the repentance of the Magdalen, passion, gloom, despair, and dawning hope in succeeding beatitude woven through the tissue of his hopes and fears as timid creator? Would the world yet ring with the mystical rhythm of his own melodies, flowing forth in mighty waves of sound? Must he be fettered down, instead, to the routine of a quiet and conscientious student, a humble, unobtrusive disciple of these great ones, like the priest born on Como in 1733, who devoted himself to severe study of counterpoint and letters?

He approached the mansion by a colonnade, and glanced into a vaulted apartment, with polished floor, and frescoed walls. A closed pianoforte stood opposite the entrance, and above it hung a picture. The work was a copy of Giorgione's trio, with the central figure of the priest, his fingers on the keys of the harpsichord, and

A World's Shrine

turned to regard the spectator with that wonderful magnetic expression in the dark eyes, in the vital portrayal of which, combined with the warm and sanguine tones of living forms, the great Venetian ranks alone.

The Abbé Liszt was once the pervading presence here. The mute piano may have responded to his touch. Giorgione's musician may have interrogated him over his shoulder, from the picture on the wall. The lake of Como belongs to Liszt in the sighing of the wind among the cypress trees, the murmur of the fountains, and the chiming unison of the church bells.

The seminarist resumed his walk, and the thread of history of his renowned predecessor was unrolled before his wistful contemplation. In the shadow of obscurity he reviewed that brilliant career. Franz Liszt was born at Raiding in 1811. His father Adam Liszt, a Hungarian, was steward on the property of Prince Esterhazy. His mother was an Austrian of modest origin. The personality of these two otherwise obscure parents has been curiously conspicuous in the century be-

A Musical Memory

cause of the lustre shed upon them by their illustrious son. Adam Liszt, the narrow, self-contained man, endowed with the artistic temperament, who had made himself familiar with all keyed instruments as well as the violin and flute, was the guardian of a prodigy, severe in discipline, and putting some method into the routine of genius, which would be sadly lacking deprived of such a mentor. The mother, gentle and mild, safe refuge of juvenile affection and caprices, coming to Paris ultimately, to furnish key-notes, in the midst of great events, of the varied development of her son under these influences. Between the sober couple stood that graceful genius the child, with his blond hair, sparkling blue eyes, sympathetic features, and tall and slender form, who won the interest and admiration of all people by his own noble Magyar nature.

On the shores of Como the fountain jet rose in the warm summer air of evening, tinged from a shaft of snowy vapour to an exquisite flush of pink in the last rays of sunshine, and the church bells began to peal forth the Angelus from every height

A World's Shrine

and inlet. The tinkling note of some chapel hidden far up among the mountains told of the childhood of Liszt. Sensitive by temperament, and excitable to all impressions, the lad was swayed to visions of the guardian angels in the distant bell of the village church. Adam Liszt, carrying a lantern, led his family along the dark country road, at the hour of the midnight mass of Christmas, to the sanctuary, where his son was dazzled by the organ, the lighted altar, and the priests, clad in gorgeous vestments, moving about amidst clouds of incense.

Other chapels in the enfolding gorges caught up, and echoed back the memory of the Bohemians, the swarthy sons of Pusta, who encamped around Raiding, and held the boy spellbound by their weird and fantastic songs and dances; the languid *Lassan*, and the agile *Frischas*.

The linked chain of melody was woven on along the crags from Val Sanagra to San Fedele and Osteno, or Val Sassina to Val di Varrone and Dervio, ringing still the refrain of this remarkable childhood. Liszt was taken to Vienna by

A Musical Memory

his father, and studied with Czerny and Salieri. In 1823 Anton Schindler, the faithful secretary of Beethoven, who deplored that the latter's genius was buried in pianoforte compositions, lured the great master to attend the concert given by Liszt at the Redoute. The boy, eleven years of age, attractive and animated, was only inspired to fresh effort under the eye of Beethoven, and played Hummel's Concerto in B flat, with a " free fantasia " afterward. Then Beethoven ascended the platform, and kissed the prodigy amidst the responsive enthusiasm of a vast multitude of an audience.

The evening bells of Como still sing this meed of praise.

Liszt went to Paris and London. Ladies petted him, and the world caressed him for his precocious talents. The fitful swelling forth and dying away of the Angelus is not more wayward than was the whimsical course of youth, now swept to a morbid prostration of shattered health, taking the phase of religious mysticism in a desire to flee from society and become a priest, sternly checked by his father, and again swaying back from inertia to energetic study, under Anton Reicha, of counterpoint and all systems of polyphony composition for several voices, the glee form and the fugue, single and double. He grasped the mysteries of the problematical canons and the canon cancrizans of the early masters. He aspired to the practice of counterpoint in such perfection of the composer as a virtuoso deems indispensable in finger drilling. The evening bells of Como, interpreted by him, alone, in his prime of years of pilgrimage, gathered volume of sound in the hamlets.

Liszt, finding in France a second fatherland, met poets, savants, and artists, was the friend of Berlioz and Chopin, even if snubbed by Cherubini on the attempt to enter the Paris Conservatoire, and pouted at by Heine. He had the noble aim ever before him of making a world acquainted with Beethoven that knew him not. He passed through the first subtle phase of sentiment by falling in love with a young French lady, his pupil. The omission to bribe the porter at the door of the paternal mansion with a five-franc piece is supposed to have changed the whole course of the musician's life. Separated from this ideal of his choice, he was plunged into an abyss of dejection and despair, from which he was aroused, and his Hungarian blood fired, by the tocsin of the Revolution of July, 1830. He sketched his *Symphonie Révolutionnaire*, which was never completed. The work was divided into three parts: the first a Sclavonic theme, a Hussite song of the fifteenth century; second, a fantasia on the German anthem *Eine feste Burg ist unser Gott;* and third, the Marseillaise. He wrote: "Gods and kings are no more; God alone remains forever, and the nations of the earth have shaken off the yoke." He turned to study with sudden and intense ardour of self-education. He was deficient in the early training of commonplace humanity. French was his natural language of polished grace in aristocratic circles, while he is reputed to have spoken German with difficulty, and his tongue to have faltered altogether in his native Magyar. He was accused of belonging to the politico-religious body of the Saint-Simonians. He was profoundly influenced by the celebrated Lamennais.

The climax in the career of Liszt was assuredly when he heard the wizard of sound, Paganini, perform in Paris in 1831. He resolved to master the pianoforte as the Italian virtuoso had mastered the violin. The theory of the future development of harmonious progress and connection of sounds dawned upon him. The final aim of both tone and harmony should consist of an increased approximation of all tones, and of all keys. Thus reasoned Liszt, an innovator, yet not wholly free from classical discipline. Paganini, as a violinist, revealed to him a new mode of technicalities for the piano, and the beautiful within the limits of subjective lyric sweetness.

The seminarist again approached the vaulted apartment, entered, opened the piano, and ran his fingers over the keys. The instrument gave forth the weak sounds of thin strings in the limited resources of the date of manufacture; an improvement on the eighteenth century and earlier

A Musical Memory

portion of the nineteenth, when Mozart, Haydn, Clementi, or Dussek failed to produce *nuances* of expression, the loud and soft phases of pedals being especially ineffective, and the quality of tone only light and smooth, yet was notably inferior to the modern grand. The intruder withdrew his hands abruptly from the keyboard. The bells gathered melody from all the lower towns of the lake shores, and floated through the mansion. They told of how Liszt gained deepest knowledge of his art, rendered all instrumentation rich and profuse in colouring, brought out new and magical effects by transposition of the principal themes and original side-themes. With him counterpoint weaving of the voice was treated in harmonious masses, melody and accompaniment moved with equal power of tone, single parts disappeared and were merged in general harmony, execution rose to the dramatic, emotion and depth of expression reached perfection. In the words of a critic of his time: "He saw in all branches of art, and especially in music, a refraction and a reflection of universal ideas, as in God's

A World's Shrine

universe. He is the most poetically complete whole of all the impressions he has received."

The praise of the united peal of the Angelus is of Liszt as a church composer. He gave to the world the Christus Oratorium, and the legend of Saint Elisabeth of Hungary.

Then a deep note welled forth from the Campanile of the Como Cathedral, in the distance, as the final stroke of this hymn to the closing day:

"His gifts were divine, but let us chant of his traits, as a man and a Hungarian, in his generous recognition of the talents of others, his charity, and his patient kindness of encouragement to timid young aspirants. Verily, such good deeds ring clear through heaven like a bell."

The priest resumed his restless walk. When he regained the house, twilight had already taken possession of the vaulted apartment, and only the olive face of Giorgione's musician glowed in the darkening canvas of the picture on the wall.

"Why do you question me with your glance when Franz Liszt has already been here?" he demanded aloud.

XVIII

A FISHERMAN

THE Como fisherman is an ancient man, withered and brown. He should be accorded a unique place in the history of humanity by the great world hurrying past his nook in battalions and armies. His career reminds one of the three wiseacres of Gotham who put out to sea in a wash-bowl, according to the nursery rhyme. He occupies the very tiniest sphere, yet is he kin to the bronzed sons of ocean of all coasts. Compared with his field of labour, the other lakes, Maggiore, Garda, or Lugano, have a vast horizon. He is entitled to a momentary consideration from the curious fact that, while the natives of many lands, both gentle and simple, may fish for minnows in a brook, either as a pastime or to supply the cottage larder with additional food, for him the

A World's Shrine

calling is a profession, followed by himself and his father before him, on this small, inland sheet of water. How wee and droll seem his ambitions as appertaining to the water populations of the earth, the African streams of mighty volume, the American network of rivers, with their tributaries, and the lakes with navigable stretches of rough billows out of sight of shores.

He lives on the side of Varenna, near the foaming cascade of the *Fiume di Latte*, where the torrent thaws in the spring, when the ice and snow begin to melt on the mountains above, winter having made the nymph of the spot a mute prisoner in crystal fetters for long months of cold in a cavern of the draughty hollow.

In the matter of living he is not better placed than the poor peasants of the Valtellina, with one room, smoky from the hearth in the middle of the floor, and the drying of chestnuts, at times, no chimney, a bed of straw on one side where sleeps the entire family, the passage way, a stable, and for protection against the wind a tattered cloth, the lamp a firebrand. On a *festa*

A Fisherman

the coarse, brown bread of daily fare is mixed with nuts divided in halves. For the rest this humble population subsists on the harvest of rivers and lakes, the fish and mollusks.

The fisherman's hovel is like those described by Virgil and Theocritus. He shares all with a comrade, a partner, as old as himself. Their couch is scarcely more than the classical rushes spread on the ground, with a bundle of dried leaves for a pillow. Nets of fine mesh and tackle are collected beneath the roof, fish-hooks attached to white horse-hair lines, poles, and baskets, osier-work for stakes and palisades in shallows. Poverty has set her seal on the premises.

Go to sea if you wish to fish, says the proverb. How is our ancient fisherman of Como to reach the sea? He haunts the side of Lecco by preference, where the river Adda, after a turbulent course down through the Valtellina range stirs the depths of Como, and flows out near the town of Lecco, then sweeps down to join the Po near Cremona. Hope is ever verdant, according

A World's Shrine

to another proverb. Why should not river Adda, as a natural gateway, bring to our fisherman riches, as well as a finny host enter Lugano in May, coming from the sea by way of the Ticino, Lake Maggiore, and the Tresa, when a party of men, on dark nights, light torches of leaves and straw, draw up their barge near shore, jump overboard to form a chain, and drive their prey to land, attracted by the fire, beating the surface of the water with oars? He patiently follows the migrations from one end of Como to the other of the palatable little fish of the herring species, the agoni. He could count on his brown fingers, if in boastful mood, the number of fine trout ever caught by him in younger days. He waits and hopes in his chances of good luck, while his boat rocks gently on the current. Who knows if there are fabulous creatures, half-monster and half-merman in the depths of the lake, such as the ancients believed in? The ledges are treacherous, and bodies of the drowned seldom recovered here. What fright if one of these shapes got entangled in the net sometime! In the

A Fisherman

meanwhile the years pass, and the boat rocks gently on the current, and the nets are often empty. Oh, that the lamprey of Crassus, or a sleek carp would rise to the hook of the ancient fisherman! He imagines he discerns strange forms down in the clear waters, such as the filmy, indeterminate polypus, the little fish of the Latins, the remora, capable of magically retarding the progress of vessels, some species of the cramp fish that benumbs the members if handled, or a modern cousin of the scarus, set free by kindred when the angler's hook has been swallowed. What if one dredged up some delicate morsel, like the naker, with a tiny lobster serving as porter at the door of the shell to watch for food? There is ever the gateway of river Adda for a shoal to approach, moving in a cube, after the manner of the tunnies, and fill his boat to overflowing, like the miracles of sacred history. He dreams of fearful adventures on stormy winter nights, when the wind makes havoc among the trees and the lake is lashed into foam. He is more apt to capture in his sleep the golden prize

A World's Shrine

of all fishermen, the magical haul which will assure fortune and ease for the remainder of life.

We are all Como fishermen, in some wise, casting our line into the lake of endless possibilities to catch the fish with golden scales of happiness or fortune. Alas! Our net too often remains empty, and the artfully baited hook does not tempt the trophy. Then we return landward at evening, weary and disheartened, to sleep on the rushes and pillow of dried leaves of bitter disappointment, hoping for better success to-morrow.

> "To-morrow and to-morrow,
> Life's but a walking shadow, a poor player,
> That struts and frets his hour upon the stage."

Vaironi of Lugano, tiny *Agoni* (*cyprinus lariensis*) of the Castle of Grato and Antiseto shore of Lecco, bearded mullet of the ponds of Lucullus and Hortensius, or golden fish of dreams of Virgil and Theocritus; humanity is ever alert to grasp the elusive prize.

XIX

THE HUMAN KEY-STONE

THE most interesting personality as a visitor to the shores of Como is the young northern architect, Saxon or Teuton. To the indifferent, casual observer he is a sympathetic character, modest, intelligent, and imbued with energy and enthusiasm to excel in his profession.

He makes his first Wanderjahre of the student in the spirit of an enjoyable vacation, and also to seek certain towns and localities, shrines of the different schools incorporated in the requirements of his calling. His sketch-book, which he carries in lieu of a traveller's diary, abounds speedily with such drawings as the transept of the Amiens Cathedral, the south portal of the Cologne Dom, a western tower of Spires, or the Strasbourg choir and crypt. He strives in his pilgrimage every-

A World's Shrine

where to gain the education of tracing the age and history of the edifice, in its manifold adaptation of usefulness. Italy, the siren, awaits him beyond the northern mountain gate of Como. He arrives, armed with all possible sobriety of judgment as to the true standards of art in contradistinction with the meretricious and false. Italy smiles and prepares to cajole him out of all practical reason by the touch of golden sunshine on her palaces, the snowy purity of moonlight on the ornate façade of temples, the mellow lustre of alabaster shaft, many-tinted marble column, and wall, brick and stucco. He is perplexed, delighted, and charmed, all in the same hour of his journeyings through the land. In conscientious parlance, he is the human key-stone that must uphold the fabric of honest and noble work in his time. A factor of modern life, he has received the training in instruction of sweeping away obstructions, and establishing wide avenues leading to some central, vast pile of buildings, thus affording a magnificent *coup d'œil* of distant effect. None the less is he prepared to in-

The Human Key-Stone

spect with reverence man's work of the past, the mysteries of intricacy in shelter of mediævalism, the screens, and shadowy aisles, and external close-grouping. Also he is alert to discern, in the first examples which meet his eye of classical architecture, the suggestion of the idea of rest in lintel and impost, as the Gothic arch and flying buttress do life and motion. He already anticipates Roman and Romanesque architecture of the thirteenth and fourteenth centuries in all simplicity and breadth of effect. He has traversed one of the passes on foot, knapsack on back and staff in hand, and descending from Chiavenna, reaches the crystal gate of Lake Como, framed by those surroundings of richly clothed hills. His dream of beauty is realised! He is south of the Alps at last!

As he gazes on the scene the lake changes with the hues of the passing hours, deepening to amber reflections and flame, the dark cypress trees mark a sharp and tapering outline amidst softer masses of verdure, and the campanili are mirrored in the surface, one by one, with the

A World's Shrine

bells hanging mute in the belfry windows, of which the wheels project far beyond the line of wall. The Basilica and Baptistery of Gravedona arrest his progress for a moment. He explores the stair-turrets in the wall, the triforium with seven arches on each side, chancel, and apsidal recesses roofed. He worships at the altar, not of the Como Cathedral as readily as the Broletto flanking it with arcaded corbels and knotted shafts. Like old Ridolfo Ghirlandajo, who loved all connected with art, and painted banners for religious processions, the standards set up at tournaments, and worked in mosaic, the young architect admires in cloister and humble sanctuary of the enfolding slopes some treasure in the shape of a chalice, enriched with blue and white enamels, and figures on stem and foot, or cross of silver filigree, *niello*, and turquoise.

Italy, the siren, sends forth her emissaries to the Como gate to receive this Northern child who should have been her son. These obey, accustomed to such missions of welcome to the stranger through all the centuries. Does the architect

The Human Key-Stone

pause over these treasures? Lo! the silver carvers and engravers flock about him from every side. Francesco Salviati, having been a goldsmith, and worker in tarsia, would fain show him how he came to the casting of small bronze figures and painting.

"Bid your modern jewellers despair when they inspect the labours of our day," quoth Benvenuto Cellini, fitting lapis-lazuli into a cruet-stand. "Look at our votive images of saints, medals, and the *niello*, or inlaid modelling-work of household furniture, sacred vessels, cups, vases, and cabinets which I tried to revive in my time. Consider the silver *palliotto* of the cathedral of Pistoja, — the paxes cut with marvellous accuracy by Pollaiuolo and Maso Finiguerra."

"True," assents the architect, musingly. The suit of armour, hanging limp on the wall of a museum acquires a deeper significance to him than the collections of weapons elsewhere. Those mighty men of valour the ancient Gauls and Romans, with thew and sinew of a different fibre surely from the human muscle as now devel-

A World's Shrine

oped, habitually wore heavy armour, and wielded morion, shield, and corselet as easily as their own limbs. Did not the Roman soldiery in the Spanish campaigns jeer at the Lacedemonians for indulging in the luxury of sleeping beneath a house roof when opportunity offered, instead of the open heavens, so inured were they to hardship? The Medes at the front of Tigranes' army, wore such weighty coverings that they were like prisoners in irons. The Parthians, on the contrary, had flexible mail which fell in scallops, as feathers fold together, yet capable of resistance to darts, while their horses were protected by leather hides.

"Link by link the coat of mail is made," soliloquises the architect, touching the embossed cuirass.

"This one might have been wrought by Leone Leoni, who executed a statue of the Emperor Charles V., and invested it with a suit of armour which could be easily taken off. The skill of Girolamo del Prato was here discernible, with equal probability, — that Girolamo who worked in

The Human Key-Stone

tarsia, inlaid metals with steel, gold, and silver, after the fashion of Damascus, and beat plates with a mallet into flexible shapes, until he achieved an entire suit of mail for a foot-soldier of Duke Alessandro de' Medici."

The architect thus roams through northern Italy, his footsteps taking him where the arts followed Goth and Longobard rule from Ravenna to Monza and Pavia in the friezes of monsters and animals, coarsely executed, the rude *bassi-relievi*, the capitals of pillars, as well as the celebrated altar-piece of San Ambrogio at Milan. Lombard doorways, piers, open porches, the tracery and moulding of trefoil ornament, string courses, voussoirs of stone, abaci of brick, the use of red, white, and grey marble together, and the fourteenth-century terra-cotta cusps of arches detain him. The Byzantine school, and those of Bologna, Florence, and Rome, in local styles, are open to him. The architects and sculptors take him by the hand to show him their task accomplished, Sansovino, Bramante, or Primaticcio. Giovan-Francesco Rustici invites him to supper

A World's Shrine

— at least in the annals of Vasari — in company of the society of the Caldron, or of the Trowel. The guests follow Ceres to the infernal regions, in quest of her daughter Proserpine, to be served with lizards, frogs, newts, toads, snakes, and gigantic spiders, by demons armed with toasting-forks, which dishes prove delicate pastry, meats, and confectionery. Giovanni da Udine familiarises the visitor with the birds and musical instruments in which he excelled, and explains how stucco decoration, such as the vaulting of the Papal Loggie, and the arches of upper tribunes, can be attained by means of gypsum, chalk, Greek pitch, wax, and pounded brick, then gilded, if one has studied the *grottesche* in very low relief discovered in the palace of Titus, in all their beauty, freshness, and profound knowledge of design, under the master Raffaello. Montorsoli eagerly displays his fountain at Messina.

Italy, the siren, cajoles and charms sober judgment.

Behold the Italian Gothic, which did not resort

The Human Key-Stone

to the buttress shaft, cusped on the under side to overcome all difficulties, and produce the trefoil arch. Behold the cornice crowning the summit of walls, campanili, porches, and running up gables, the mellow tones of brickwork and stone in church and shafted cloister. Is not the result sometimes gained by audacity, seeming carelessness and indolence, even, in breaking standard rules of harmony to serve the aim of the moment, fair enough, surrounded by the beauty of the land and crystallised by the purity of climate? If he visits the tombs of the Scaligers at Verona a market is held at the base, with awnings and cotton umbrellas spread over heaps of fruit and vegetables. If he lingers near the Lucca monuments, sculptured, inlaid, and diapered in precious marbles, a local *festa* of a Saint's day lends life and animation to the scene. The Tuscan springtime has such elements for his eye as, when contemplating the vast pile of the Florence Duomo, the funeral procession of an archbishop wends about the temple, with banners, gilded crosses, gold and velvet canopies, tapers, and white-robed

A World's Shrine

priests. The balcony, with moulded beams, and groining in transverse, and diagonal ribs of an ancient castle, half farmhouse in decay, and adjacent doorway with traces of fresco in the tympanum, which he transfers to his sketch-book, standing on the other side of the paved way of a little hamlet, holds beauty, radiant, softly tinted, smiling; the woman at the window who is the bunch of grapes of the roadside, to quote the national proverb. His casement studies, wheels divided by shafts and little columns, set in blocks of stone, with plate tracery, or having terra-cotta capitals, are sadly interfered with by the charming heads of youth, in all types of blonde and brunette, peeping out at him, roguishly, a snatch of song on the lips:

> "Now blessings on Matteo's kindly art!
> He's made a window after my own heart;
> He has not made it me too low nor high,
> And so I see my love when he goes by."

"Return when your Northern skies are dull, and all the colour of sunshine you know comes through the painted glass of your Cathedrals," mocks Italy.

The Human Key-Stone

"We always return," sighs the architect.

Once more Como towers are mirrored in the tranquil waters, and the bells hang mute, as he takes his way over the mountain pass. Everywhere he encounters the human key-stone on his route, the manhood of fair seeming that will crumble at the first shock of adversity, the specious gilded stucco presented to the world's gaze of Giovanni da Udine or the solid foundations of honesty of the great Masters. Time, the Architect, will also test this disciple as he takes up his career, whether he designs the sky in his dome, the rocks for columns, or wreathes his cornices and capitals with decorations of olive, laurel, and acanthus leaves.

THE SEASONS

I

WINTER

XX

A PATRIARCHAL VILLA

THE villa was small and modest, with a tiny garden surrounded by a high wall on either side, and a boat moored at the flight of steps. Situated on a bay of the western bank, the hill rises in an overhanging cliff in the rear, with paths winding among the olive trees to the heights. The place was not only unpretentious in comparison with the castellated and ornate surburban palaces of the vicinity, but bore evidence of age in the fading tones of the painted walls, narrow embrasures, and dilapidated roof and cornice. Such as it was the villa represented a little paradise to the owner, and was endeared by many associations. Not for any consideration would he have spent the late autumn and early winter in any other spot.

A World's Shrine

The habitation, in its severe simplicity, might have reminded the visitor of the retreat of Gallus, whose house came within the span of the shelter of a single pine tree, while the thatch of the roof covered only one story. Like this Roman prototype, the Como retreat sufficed for the inmate's *villeggiatura* if one guest partook with him of the fruit of the vine, the lupin which flourished in his garden patch, and the loaf of bread baked in the domestic oven. Was this little? Gallus demanded no greater luxury. Even more was the proprietor like Tranquillus, who sought his country property in the autumn, far from Rome, where the course of life flowed smoothly and monotonously. In the present case Gallus and Tranquillus have their typical representative in the Lombard gentleman. He was a noble by birth, and his family had tenanted the land of Como for centuries, numbering prelates, poets, historians, and statesmen in the ranks. He was a stanch patriot in all public interests, but he was first a Lombard before an Italian, speaking the local dialect by preference.

A Patriarchal Villa

He resided in the brilliant capital of Milan in bachelor quarters scarcely less restricted than the rural home, and supplemented the shrunken fortunes of his race by filling a government office. He mingled in polished circles, and was a dilettante in art and music. He belonged to clubs and literary societies, which furnish the modern equivalent of the mediæval Academy della Crusca of Florence, the Noctes Vaticanæ of Rome, the Men of Virtue and Fame, or the Vineyard, the Cask, the Frogs, and the Eels of other towns, where members wrangled, and discussed the merits of contemporaries, possibly with as much perspicacity as Petrarch and Tasso were criticised in their day. The guest of the Como villa might be a famous savant, a sculptor of renown, an improvisator of graceful wit, or a popular actor.

Several cabinets and coffers of antique wood-carving, Venetian and Tuscan, contained the treasures of plate and porcelain of the mansion; portraits of ancestors, time-stained and dilapidated, adorned the interior. The ample personality of a bishop, reputed to have wielded two pens, one of iron, and one of gold, to please his patrons the Pope Leo X. and Clement VII., seemed to listen to the conversation that transiently animated the desertion of the Patriarchal Villa. A courtier, in a velvet doublet, who found favour with Francis I. and Charles V. in his time, smiled at the sallies of a modern diplomatist, while a poet who attended the Council of Trent slightly frowned at a Latin quotation made glibly by a clever journalist. For living audience the old domestic Antonio, given charge of the premises, as a sort of honourable retirement from active duties, also listened in serving the supper, with keen and intelligent appreciation of the topics discussed. He gossiped with the gardener of the next property, indicating the visitor of the date with a jerk of the thumb over his shoulder.

"Eh! he talks like a printed book, an oracle, an old man. You should have heard him last evening."

The Lombard gentleman had firm faith in the

A Patriarchal Villa

soothing and recuperative virtues of native air. His fountain of Egeria to ward off decrepitude in advancing years was a daily bath in the transparent waters of the lake; to climb the hillside and ramble through the vineyards; and to labour in his little garden, fostering and experimenting on rare plants. The enclosure boasted palms, Chinese pines, camellias, and roses that braved the winter, sheltered by the wall. An amateur horticulturist, full of zeal on his holiday, he had cultivated robinia, catalpa, acacia, and bignonia successfully. Floral triumphs might yet be in store for him with a minister of agriculture in the perfecting of chrysanthemums to balls of snow or tufts of copper plumes, orchids of eccentric convolutions of growth and bloom, and tawny or vivid emerald depths, gigantic violets of marvellous sweetness, and double heartease in rich tones of velvety purple and amethyst.

When he arrived, the old Antonio said to the neighbours:

"The master is as dry as a herring, after the town, and yellow as a pumpkin, as saffron, or the

A World's Shrine

gold of a zechin. You will see what the villeggiatura does for his health."

Autumn winds blew away the dried leaves, and the old Gallus found a tonic to his blood in the frosty morning air, even if the hearth at evening required to be heaped with the resinous wood that emitted a fragrant smoke. The ground was ploughed and sown for the winter grain. Then came December, crisp and sparkling, and with the opening of January a new phase of splendour to the lake world. Colour does not appertain to summer alone in this realm. The water has deep tints of malachite green shading to cold, steely blue reflections, the peaks are dazzling citadels of fresh snow on a clear sky, and the intervening hills one solid bloom of mingled hues, robbed of the veil of soft, atmospheric haze of heat. All day that rampart of Splügen and Stelvio range is a field for the kaleidoscopic play of light and shadow, swept by the *tramontano*, pale amber and opal in the early rays of the sun, resplendent in deeper gold, with glistening crags of glacier revealed in the sombre gulf of descending preci-

A Patriarchal Villa

pices, and masses of ice formed about every cavern fissure of lower slopes, blanched to chalky whiteness at noon, and gathering again all the fleeting changes of the setting sun in a transient glow of rose and crimson, until quenched to wan and spectral sentinels, wrapped in majestic draperies of winter beneath the stars. Frost had stiffened the palm fronds so that they rattled in the wind with a brittle sound, the olives acquired a tint of aqua marine, and the blackened berries sparkled with frozen water-drops as if enclosed in crystal. In the tiny garden the stems of certain plants gleamed like branches of coral, icicles hung about the fountain basin, and a misty thaw on leaf and branch made little diamond and topaz filaments of fringes.

The Lombard had witnessed the great drama of the sunrise, when Phœbus saluted Eos, the Dawn. His last guest was the Piedmontese, and they had gone forth among the hills, with guns slung over the shoulder in pursuit of the hare. In the evening they paused in the garden to contemplate the amphitheatre of mountains. The

A World's Shrine

Piedmontese repeated slowly the poem of Queen Margherita to the Madonna of the Snows for the soldiers in peril on the Alps: —

"O Virgin Mother of God, invoked by the mountaineer as the Madonna of the eternal snows! O Lady of the high mountains, turn your gaze towards the white expanse that seems a portion of your veil in purity, so immaculate is it, and mitigate the horrors of the route to those in danger."

Then the proprietor of the patriarchal villa returned to town life. Antonio limped about the premises closing shutters and chambers once more.

"The master goes back as plump as a thrush, a *beccafico*, an ortolan," quoth the old servant.

THE SEASONS

II
SPRING

XXI

BLOSSOMS

THE artist came with the earliest flush of spring that tinged the foliage and grassy banks of Como. She was no radiant Flora, with flowing tresses and gossamer draperies, her basket filled with violets, primrose, and daffodil, but a plain woman, sunburned from exposure to all weathers, wearing a short gown of serviceable woollen stuff, stout boots, and a straw hat which would have been deemed inexcusable by the censors of fashionable millinery.

She was welcomed by the people, old and young, having for all the pleasant sympathy of the fraternity. Her early flight to the lake shores was like the advent of the first swallows, a harbinger of the budding season. The children made themselves willing guides to spots where

A World's Shrine

favourite flowers grew, because she sought them with a characteristic environment of the gnarled roots of an adjacent tree, a moist nook of brown soil, a tuft of grasses and ferns, a bit of overhanging rock, stained with a patch of lichens, or a glimpse of blue sky visible through a low-sweeping branch of glancing leaves, and did not wish to receive whole sheaves of half-faded trophies dragged up by the roots with the misguided zeal of ruthless little hands. She soon evaded these attendants, and made her pilgrimage alone. To the inner eye of spiritualised perception, at least, the iris above the cataract was ever forming and dissolving in the play of colour here. Nature, in a benevolent if mocking mood commanded, "Follow me."

The artist obeyed, dazzled, fascinated, even bewildered by the wealth of beauty lavished about her. She endeavoured to catch some weak, crude, and fleeting impression of the floral rainbow spanning this Eden in the time of blossoms. Her little porcelain palette resembled the plate dappled with paints given by Turner to the children to

Blossoms

mingle into new combination of tints by the play of their fingers. Sweeter to the visitor in subtle intuition than human smiles and voices was the salutation of the children of the earth.

"You arrive too late this year," sighed the almond, shedding a few rosy petals down on her head.

"We have waited for you," said the hardy winter rose, nestling in the hollows of the mountain side.

"Ah! There you are!" chimed the crocus, starring the turf with white flowers, and thin, silky lilac buds.

The tiny bog violets peeped out at her, shyly, from the sides of ravines, while the anemones, of a brownish purple hue, wrapped in down hoods, added a welcome.

The warm winds prevailed, steeping all the senses in languor, and the sun shed down rays of heat, loosening the tongue of every babbling torrent descending from icicle and glacier above. Showers were abundant, in turn, when in the opinion of the farmer each drop of rain that falls

A World's Shrine

in April is worth a hundred francs. The vines formed cables of verdure, looped from tree to tree; stalks of early wheat had sprung up in vivid, emerald freshness between the olive terraces, flecked with poppies; and tangled creepers clung to the slope down to the cactus and aloe boundary of gardens along the shore. The artist trod the woods carpeted with amaranth and genista. The fruit trees made fairy pavilions over her in which to dream through long hours: the snowy canopy of the wild cherry, sprays of the deep magenta of the Judas tree, a pink tent of peach blossoms, the white of pear and apricot, and fragrant nespoli. The lines of care were smoothed from her hard-favoured, energetic features, her mouth relaxed into soft smiles, and snatches of song escaped, unconsciously, from her lips. She experienced an elasticity of spirit similar to that of George Sand when the great writer was able to abstract herself from humanity and lived in the plants, the grass, the clouds, the flowing stream, as a tree-top, or a bird. Then the artist's mood would acquire a tinge of more serious thought. She was

Blossoms

aware that she must return to a work-a-day world when her holiday was over. In the meanwhile she contemplated, not only the waves upon waves of bloom, rippling overhead, and lining her path, red stalk, scarlet leaflets on the tips of branches, yellow and purple masses, fit to offer on the altar of a sun-goddess, a screen of soft, perfumed rose-hued and deep orange splendour, here and there, but was aware of the mysterious processes of development going on silently in the ground to produce such results.

Then the golden broom beckoned her on among the hills, where silver hawthorn, jonquils, hyacinths, laburnum, and columbine grew, up to the sphere of gentian and white asphodel, with unexpected curves dipping gently down to foster beds of lilies-of-the-valley, sprinkling the air delicately with sweetness from their liliputian bells. These, also, whispered to her their secrets, spurning their swaddling-clothes of calyx, and uprearing the life germ, the corolla, to the day. She questioned each chalice, noting the depths of blue clouding, mauve, and violet, with mottled

A World's Shrine

streaks and dashes of flame and pearl about the stamens.

The artist bade farewell to her paradise, and returned to a studio on a narrow street of a sombre town, where smoke from factory chimneys hung heavy over the roofs. She opened her sketch-book, and store of paints. For the rest of the year spring blossoms signified the judicious use of carmine and madder for flowers, chromes, ochres, and cobalt in designing sprays of peach and almond across screens, panels, and even in the bread winning of dainty devices in artistic advertisement. She had been with the butterflies, wasps, and dragon-flies; now she must emulate the sober bee in making and storing honey. Not high art? If she does her best at the task allotted by fate who has the right to criticise? Even within town limits she belongs to the *plein air* school.

THE SEASONS

III

SUMMER

XXII

A CONCEITED SNAIL

THE summer noonday on Como is hushed, and of a fiery intensity. The absolute sway of midday is supreme. Butterflies flit, like blossoms blown fitfully, among the plants, and an occasional bee hums as if drowsy with sunshine. The dry, monotonous chirp of the cicada is the key-note of sultry heat. Threads of golden light penetrate the meshes of stems and boughs, and weave a tissue through the foliage of warm shadow, which furnish a web of reverie, fancies, dreams.

The great man had retired to yonder spacious villa, with many casements, architectural adornments, works of art, and chapel. He had a grievance, and Como is a delightful spot in which to sulk at the world. He had a bald head, a

A World's Shrine

thick nose, and a squeaky voice, but he was a very illustrious personage, at least in his own estimation. He had been unjustly dealt with by contemporaries. In the government of country, and the veering of the international weather-cock of the moment he was in favour of a British, French, or Russian alliance at the wrong juncture. A sharp altercation with the leader of the opposition ensued, in which much eloquence of sarcasm was expended on both sides. He imagined that royalty frowned on him. The only course was to withdraw from the active arena, and be missed. Was his absence deplored by any one? Other favourites rose to popularity. He was like the Roman patrician who was incensed at the intrusion of Senators from Gaul under Julius Cæsar. He was a modern Umbricius, withdrawn from the capital to Cumæ in dudgeon, because of the number of polished and adroit Greeks usurping all posts. He also might exclaim: " Shall that man take precedence of me, who came to Rome with a cargo of plums and figs? Is it of no account that my infancy drew the breath

A Conceited Snail

on the Aventine, and was nurtured on the Sabine olive berry?"

As the Romans of the Republic vaunted their own honesty and truthfulness, with *Fides* for their motto, in contrast with the mendacity of the Greeks and the perfidy of the Phœnicians, so did he pride himself on a probity not shared by all of his countrymen. He took as models Fabricius, or the incorruptible Regulus and Cincinnatus.

Truly each world revolves on itself, as well as around a centre. Ambition is a trait averse to solitude; the great man, therefore, did not willingly taste of the sleepy flood of oblivion by the stream of Lethe to which he had retired.

He seated himself in a *chaise longue* of a cool portion of the garden, with a carafe of wine and another of water on an adjacent marble table, and opened a fresh journal.

"Cripples are very unfit for exercises of the body, and lame souls for exercises of the mind," said a sage.

Thus the recluse perused a political leader,

A World's Shrine

fumed, shook his head, and tossed aside the obnoxious sheet. In Italian parlance he became as red as a pepper, as a cherry, as a shrimp, or an iron heated in the fire. He rose, and took several turns on the path soliloquising and gesticulating at the latest act of folly of the ministry, then stretched himself once more in the chair, raised his slippered feet from the ground in a comfortable pose, and spread a silk handkerchief over his bald head. The next moment he uttered a snore. The box hedges exhaled a pungent scent, the pines and cedars breathed a resinous fragrance in the hot air, mingled with aromatic and sweet odours from shrubbery and flowers. The cicadas, shrilling in the leafy thickets, made a rural orchestra of glassy, rasping sounds, now in chorus and duets, and again in solos, — a stridulous, drowsy concert. This was the summer hynm of the sun and labour, while the fruit garnered juices, and the grain turned to gold.

"Hush! The god Pan sleeps at noon," said a yellow butterfly.

"If he is the god Pan I have half a mind to

A Conceited Snail

tickle his nose and wake him," buzzed a fly that had been trotting on the table, tasting a drop of spilled wine.

"Let the creature doze if he can," pleaded the amiable butterfly. "See me waltz with the flowers," and the insect flitted in mazy circles amidst the roses and lilies.

"Is it a skirt dance? I can glide around, if you like," said the little snake, advancing stealthily at the base of a stone wall, broken and moss-grown.

The snail approached slowly on the margin of bank. Does a snail creep, or waddle? This one traversed a given space of ground in its own fashion. Here was no sinuous shell of pearly hue within, with lustre imbibed in the sun's palace porch, but a somewhat battered relic, shabby and knocked about, of sea-life at some remote period, and the door of the mansion fitted snugly. The inmate was plump, not to say portly, as if the fine appetite of eating an eighth part of its own weight of cabbage in three hours, attributed to the species, was verified in this Como garden.

A World's Shrine

The snail had all the egotism of Montaigne's Gosling, and deemed itself the very centre of the universe. A scorpion, in form a small cray-fish, emerged from a fissure of the wall.

"Come over here, snail, where the ground is nice and moist," said the scorpion in an affable tone.

"Please don't hurry me," protested the snail. "Besides, I know all the best places. This garden belongs to me, and has always been in my family."

The tiny ant folk, busy with their own affairs, paused to listen, waving antennæ in the air; a brown beetle, clambering up a hillock of loose soil, rolled over on its back with laughter at the superb statement, and the grasshoppers, skipping here and there in the turf—for it was true grasshopper weather—giggled. The pretty snake glided nearer, and added:

"The song of the children from France, Italy, Germany, and Russia to China is the same:

> 'Snail, Snail, put out your horn,
> Or I'll kill your father and mother the morn.'"

A Conceited Snail

The Como mollusk obeyed, exclaiming:

"Goodness! Are there children about? That is the worst of being so tender and delicate, you know. Everybody wishes to eat you."

"Succulent," suggested the scorpion, waggishly. "Ho! ho! I might be taken for a *bonne bouche.*"

"Never!" replied the snail in a tone of condescension. "You are quite safe. Who ever heard of eating a scorpion? Now for my part it makes me shudder to consider those suppers of Lucullus where dressed snails were indispensable, or the snailery of Prince Esterhazy in Hungary where my kindred are fattened on favourite plants. I think I am an Anglomaniac because the English speaking races, as a rule, are squeamish about adopting us for food. The Latin nations are not to be depended on. The French emulate the ancient Romans in culinary skill of serving me up. Great ladies may still surfeit themselves on a dainty as Maria Bianca Sforza, wife of Maximilian I., is said to have injured her health. There is a brisk trade going on between the Valtellina and Bergamo in large snails at present."

"Is it true that the French make syrups and lozenges of *escargots* for nervous maladies?" mocked the little snake.

"Is it true that you eat fennel to render your eyes bright, and attract birds, according to Pliny?" retorted the snail, tartly.

The snake raised its head, and hissed angrily.

"You belong to a very large family, I believe," said a cicada, looking down from a branch with goggle eyes.

"Oh, yes," said the snail, yawning, and preparing to shut the door for a *siesta*. "The gasteropodous mollusk, the vertigo, with a cylindrical, fusiform shell, the Limax, a slug, and the *Paludina vivipara* of fresh-water pools are relatives of mine."

"Well! if I ever saw a conceited snail," said the scorpion.

"What did you say?" demanded the object of criticism, suspiciously.

"Oh, nothing," rejoined the scorpion.

A Conceited Snail

The hot air seemed to have vibrations in the chirp of the insects, mingled with a soporific hum in the distance of slower wings.

"Hush! The god Pan sleeps at noon," repeated the yellow butterfly, poising on a spray of jasmine.

Thereupon the mischievous fly tickled the nose of the great man. A stout lady in a loose, white robe, with her abundant, dark hair beautifully coiffed, appeared at a door of the closed mansion.

"My friend, you will get an apoplexy out there in the heat," she warned.

"True," assented the great man, rising and testing the temperature of his brow, anxiously.

A stroke of apoplexy would be a sad calamity to the political world.

"Did you mean a conceited snail?" inquired the little snake of the scorpion.

"If the cap fits," replied the scorpion, withdrawing into the fissure of wall once more.

THE SEASONS

IV

AUTUMN

XXIII

HIS OWN VINE AND FIG-TREE

ON the outskirts of a hamlet of the western bank of Como, between Gravedona and Colico, stands a wayside *osteria* of modest pretensions. The road is usually white with dust, the inn small, as a resort of refreshment from the heat, and consists of two rooms on the ground-floor, with several additional, irregular chambers, gained by a ladder-like stairway, under the roof of crimped and fluted brown tiles. The house is coloured a warm saffron pink hue, the shutters of the small windows are yellowish green, and vines of the striped gourd climb around the upper casements in a not ungraceful canopy of leaves.

A niche above the door holds a statuette of the Madonna of terra-cotta in a robe of deep,

A World's Shrine

hard blue. The gate which encloses garden patch, and a few fruit trees, is wide open on the arid highway, as if inviting a thirsty wayfarer to enter. The approach to the habitation is characteristic of northern Italy and the Tyrol, the work of the kitchen being turned out-of-doors, as it were, in an easy, unkempt fashion. Fowls peck about the threshold, and pigeons strut on the roof. The Grandmother Agata shells peas or beans in an earthen basin, or washes salad and vegetables on the bench placed along the wall, while the buxom mistress of the premises rinses linen, dresses small fish, or attends to other culinary preparations in view of possible customers, the actual triumph of frying or roasting belonging to the skill of the host, with his one arm. The *osteria* faces the lake, with an arbour (pergola) leading in the direction of the water, covered with luxuriant grapevine, and a strip of shingle along the shore where boats may push up on occasion.

A rustic simplicity pertains to the little inn, yet it is a shrine with a history sufficiently complete to have rounded the sphere of experience to the participants.

The charming custom has long prevailed of having Manzoni's *Promessi Sposi* performed at the town of Lecco, each season, by a good dramatic company. In how many nooks of Como the drama may be enacted in real life, with each new generation!

The pedestrian tempted to seek simple fare and enter the *osteria* is welcomed with an easy grace of courtesy that any Boniface might envy. Leandro, the host, a sun-bronzed man, with a frank and good-humoured physiognomy, a vigorous, muscular figure, and an empty sleeve where a stalwart right arm should serve him through life, invites the stranger to be seated at a table under the pergola, shaded by the canopy of green vine-leaves, and breakfast on a dish of eggs, fish of the lake, or a *stufato* (stew), and a morsel of Gorgonzola cheese; the repast completed by a flask of sound wine (*vino sincero*).

Laura, the hostess, assists in these preparations. She is a handsome young woman, with

A World's Shrine

a sympathetic face, a true daughter of autumn sunshine and the lake district in the warm tones of skin, and the supple outline of throat, shoulder, and bust. Her black hair is braided in tresses and surrounded by an aureole of silver pins, while coral beads and filigree of gold encircle her neck. Her dark eyes look out from beneath level brows with a steadfast expression. Probably the stranger, keenly observant of types in foreign lands, will wonder where such girls of the people obtain their proud bearing, finely moulded limbs, and noble features.

The Grandmother Agata, bent, careworn, and wrinkled, knitting a stocking, will pause beyond the entrance of the arbour, looking on, like St. Anna in the background of the altar pictures of the early masters. The children gather near the decrepit fig-tree at the angle of the house, with the house dog, a mastiff of sagacious aspect, whose bearing to customers is bland at this hour.

If the stranger is affable, as tourists are apt to be in such places, he elicits the modest history

A Como Girl

His own Vine and Fig-tree

of the group before him, as easily as he would read the page of an open book. Indeed Leandro, the host, with the dramatic instinct of his race, rehearses the whole to an attentive listener.

Yes, he is master here, at last! Like Manzoni's hero Renzo he is an orphan, and inherited this bit of land (*a poderetto*), where he would have gladly dwelt, and tended his own fruit trees. He is a *contadino* by nature, honest, peaceable, and temperate; but the conscription swept him away to the irksome military career, and later he went to Africa. Bello! The Signore finds him as black as a Moor. The sun down there burns. He was affianced to Laura yonder. How they have waited! The couple look at each other and smile. If Leandro was wont in those careless days of the earliest youth to troll songs beneath the humble casement of his mistress, in a fine baritone voice, declaring the girl to be a blossom of the peach, a flower of the mint, the gourd, the radish, or her mouth as sweet as the grapes when the vintage is ripest, Laura may now retort, demurely:

A World's Shrine

> "When I was a maiden free and blithesome,
> Of Strombotti I knew a bushel.
> Married now, no more so blithesome,
> This bushel's o'erturned and spilt away."

Here the Grandmother Agata nods and changes her knitting-needles with nimble fingers. Yes, the Laura was faithful, and waited for the soldier to return. She had many other suitors. A fine girl like that, and of good character! What would you have? Why, even the superintendent of the silk mill at Bergamo — eh! — but no, she made a vow to the Madonna that she would marry Leandro, or no one.

Leandro resumes the thread of his often repeated experiences. He was stationed at Massaua; he was at Dogali; missing; given up for dead; hidden from the enemy until nearly starved; then succeeded in crawling back to camp, and had his wounded right arm amputated. He ultimately regained native shores, and home. What did he find? The cousin who had promised to take care of his little property had died, and the family emigrated. His betrothed and her mother

His own Vine and Fig-tree

had moved to Bergamo in search of work in the silk mills. The modern soldier, like his mediæval prototype of the famous romance, inspected his domain in dismay. No barrier gate remained, and the people of the country had rifled everything they could carry off, — mulberries, figs, and cherries. New growth of shoots and creepers weighed down the branches, and strove to stifle each other by a prodigal, untrammelled luxuriance. The ground was covered with a mass of weeds, ferns, tares, cockles, grass, wild-oats, green amaranth, tangled roots, sorrel, and dock; the noxious intruders abhorred by the husbandman of all lands. A wilderness of plants braided, climbed, and twisted in a confusion of leaves, flowers, and fruit of varied colours, sprays of red and white, stars of blue blossoms, and bunches of yellow bloom. The bramble held full sway, linking its stem from one neighbour to another, dipping down earthward, then clambering up beyond, and disputing the passage of all intruders. The fig-tree still stood, and several mulberries, with the gourd vine running riot

A World's Shrine

among the branches. The grape, vigorous and untrained, triumphed over this waste of fragrance, and spread green leaves, flowers, and clusters of purple fruit on the trellis of the pergola. The harvest was rudely despoiled, as Manzoni describes the Spanish soldiery entering the vineyards around Lecco, and saving the peasants the trouble of any vintage. This Renzo also forced his way through the matted weeds, and entered the house. Storms had mildewed the walls, spiders spun webs across the ceiling, and mice had taken possession of the premises. A worthy comrade found him here, inert and despairing, cheered him by a good welcome, made a fire on the hearth, put on the pot of water to heat and stir in the maize for *polenta*, then brought the little *secchio* of milk, a bit of bacon, a couple of *raveggioli* (goat's-milk cheese), figs, and peaches. Thus comforted by human fellowship, Leandro had sought and found his affianced bride. The wedding had been performed by the parish priest, a sleek Don Abbondio, who fills his sphere benevolently, although he may be an earthen vase

His own Vine and Fig-tree

amidst the iron vessels of humanity in the community. Laura had worn her bodice of brocade, and sleeves fastened with ribbons, and brought a modest dowry of household linen, saved from her wages. Her cheeks had not lost their bloom, nor her eyes their brilliancy in the waiting. Don Abbondio often sits in the shade of the pergola, takes a pinch of snuff, and questions the children. Also a capuchin with a silvery beard, in a brown robe, and sandals, who makes a quest for his community with a coarse bag carried over his shoulder, receives from Laura her apron full of chestnuts. He might be own brother of Fra Cristoforo of long ago. He had prayers repeated in the convent chapel for a safe return of Leandro by the intercession of the Virgin, and even wrote letters to the absent one.

"It is only by a miracle of the Madonna I am here, at all, after that blessed Africa," concludes the host of the little inn.

The October day glorifies all nature, filling the ravines in the cliffs across the lake with a golden mist, touching the surface of the ripples with a

A World's Shrine

light breeze that imparts a silvery green tint of the beryl to the mid-current, and all merging to the amber, russet, and rich brown of distant reaches of shore, like molten metal in the warm atmosphere. Zones of foliage, ivy, and brushwood, withered to yellow and grey tones by autumn, cover lower slopes of undulating ridges, crags clothed with sombre firs rise above, and heights are bathed in rose, lilac, and blue, melting to the delicacy of a pearly horizon. All is peaceful in the sunshine; the rough winds sleep, and winter storms seem far away beyond the mighty Alpine rampart. This poem of gaiety, reverie, passionate animation, and indolence, the life of the native, goes on through the centuries almost unchanged, while light and shadow pass over the peaks, little hamlets gleam out on upper spurs here and there, and a church tower glistens set in the mass of verdure of a gorge, sending the note of its bell in greeting down to the boats.

Beyond the pergola a vat half-filled with grapes is trodden by two naked boys, as pretty as cherubs, with much roguish glee. The youth-

His own Vine and Fig-tree

ful Bacchanals, the sons of Leandro, like the cupids of a Greek vase, afford a key-note of the scene and the land.

The maimed soldier has returned home to dwell under his own vine and fig-tree. What greater boon could he ask of providence? To own his grapes, and make wine is the fulfilment of well-being to Leandro. He cherishes, prunes, enriches, and trims the roots and tendrils with personal care. Woe betide the wild boar of a marauder capable of ruthlessly trampling this vineyard with the legitimate owner once more in possession! The most sheep-like native waxes fierce in defence of his harvest before the vintage throughout the land. Leandro watches, spies, and remains wakeful day and night. He looses the mastiff with stern injunctions to give no quarter to thieves, acts as sentinel himself, gun in hand, and would plant a howitzer on the strip of beach if he could, to intimidate intruders. Who knows? An honest neighbour may be tempted to rifle a basket of grapes, and make a little wine in his own cellar. As for thirsty ur-

A World's Shrine

chins, gazing wistfully at the tempting bunches swinging out of reach on the pergola, like the fox of the fable, they need to be taught a severe lesson at this season.

Pliny the Younger, in his praise of various pergolæ could have commended the exuberance of growth of Leandro's inheritance. The note-taking Roman gentleman might readily have pronounced the vine of the modest Inn: *Una vitis Romæ in Liviæ porticibus pergulis opacat eadem duodenis musti amphoris fœcunda*, etc.

Leandro is a temperate man withal, yet his own wine is as the nectar of the gods to him. What would Pliny, acquainted with many varieties of grapes for the table and vintage, have thought of Leandro's wine? Would the beverage not have been deemed thin and acid, sadly lacking in body and bouquet, resembling the Setine wine preferred by Augustus, the Veientine, or that of Varenna and Griante, recommended to Lodovico Sforza for his health? The wise Pliny must have interrogated this rustic son of Como, born so many generations after himself, thus:

His own Vine and Fig-tree

"By what process, O brother, do you extract the juice of the grapes? According to the most ancient methods, when libations were first poured out to the gods, and men under thirty years of age, as well as all women, were forbidden to drink it, the fruit was gathered in osier baskets, squeezed by the press, the *torculum*, or *prelum*, the liquid passed through a strainer, and received in a tub, or vat of masonry work, lined with plaster, and sunk in the ground, or put in a large cask of wood, the *dolium*, or even potter's earth, until fermentation was over. The must, or new wine, refined by mixture with the yolk of pigeon's eggs, was poured into vessels (amphoræ), covered with pitch, or chalk, and bunged. Wine was even kept in leather bags. Do you make the Passum wine of half-dried grapes? Do you mellow your vintage over smoke in a fumarium, or give a flavour of rosin, on occasion? Of course, poor man, there is no question of serving your customers in jugs, with two handles, glass, precious amethyst cups, murrha, or the ware of Samos. One does as one can in this world!

A World's Shrine

Possibly you buy your wine in casks, or amphoræ, from the public depositories after the Roman custom."

The jolly Leandro would have responded:

"I just heap my bruised fruit into a hogshead, and am lucky if it comes out fit for barrel or flask in time."

He awaits custom within his own boundaries, but he attends fairs occasionally, where he meets many comrades, and is required to narrate over again his adventures on the Red Sea. An annual *festa* suffices for him. His Ham Fair of the Paris Easter, or summer fête of Neuilly, may be no more than a Saint's day in September when gifts are blessed in a favourite church, rabbits, doves, pomegranates, olive oil, and pears.

Autumn steeps the hills in haze, the lake surface changes like a jewel from frosted emerald and sapphire to golden reflections as the sky warms to the glowing radiance of the waning day. The withered leaves of the grape vine flutter down through the trellis of the Pergola on the head of Leandro, whose contented mood is undisturbed. He exclaims:

"*Casa mia, casa mia, per piccina che tu sia, tu mi sembri una badia.*"

(Oh, my own house, however small, seems to me as spacious as an abbey.)

XXIV

BOYHOOD

CARLO entered the chestnut woods. The place was his kingdom, his world. He was too young to dream of any other sphere. Ambition still slumbered in his breast. Military conscription, or emigration might sweep him away from the home nook, and make a man of him. The boy had never thought about the matter. The chestnut wood had represented life from the cradle to the grave to so many generations. Why need he go further in his time? This son of Como was as nearly akin to sylvan creatures, and the shepherds as civilised humanity may well be. The ignorant simplicity of a healthy young animal amply sufficed at this period of existence. On the other hand the gifts of chance could as readily be showered upon him. Fancy

Boyhood

deals with his lot, according to the hour and the season. He was a connecting link of the races of the south, between the remote past of Italy and Greece and the present of the farm villa labourer. Now we relegate him readily to the Arcadians of Virgil. The lad was neither clumsy nor loutish in bearing, although he did not know how to read or write. He was well formed and firmly coloured. In adolescence he would serve as a model for an artist, moving with the easy grace of untrammelled limbs, and inspired with the naïve vanity of his people. In Arcadia the description of him would have been that his flesh was white as cheese, and his frame as delicate as that of a lamb; only, he possessed the glorious strength of a young bull, and the firmness of a green grape. The melodies of his little reed pipe must have discoursed about the changing of Narcissus into a flower, and hiding Daphne within the bark of a tree. His songs, as a Corydon, dealt with the beech thickets, the clumps of alder, the green laurel, and tender myrtles; of Thestylis crushing together the garlic with the fragrant wild thyme, and other plants more bitter than the herbs of Sardinia. Offerings to a shepherdess consisted of plums as yellow as wax, the peach with velvet down, apples, and the golden marigold.

On the prosaic side of real life Carlo was only a simple lad, with ear attuned to the strident note of the cicada in the heat, the murmur of bees, and the occasional call of the hawk wheeling through the luminous atmosphere in flight towards the Stelvio. As a baby he was brought in the cradle to the chestnut wood with the rest of the family, and carefully minded by the dog while the others worked. Such was his baptism of experience received from the foster-mother, the grove, and under the watchful eye of canine wisdom. Sunny years succeeded, of light-hearted mischief and gaiety, scrambling early on nimble, little legs, to toddle after the older children in sport or labour. The down of those first seasons was still on this nestling. No book lore was his, and he struggled fiercely to escape thraldom of schooling as the wild creatures hid amidst the branches and rocky ledges, but he read the page daily outspread before the quick eye of urchinhood. The young marauder, with dusky cheeks, a ready smile, and white teeth, exemplified the proverb that a goat was never known to die of hunger. Carlo was familiar with the dells where a scanty harvest of edible berries ripened, and the pine-tree of the ravine that yielded the seed-like kernels from the cones, as well as the field of fungus growth. Precocious alertness marked his skill in snaring birds with willow twigs, and a noose of string baited with red berries. Such luck as catching the quail, weary with the flight from Africa, in nets attached to poles was scarcely to be hoped for, but a careless lark, or a thrush might, at any time, hop his way. The chestnuts appeased the cravings of hunger for a considerable portion of the year. In conformity with the adage he ate the bread of the woods, and drank the wine of the clouds. No dulness of spirit, or lack of imagination characterised his rustic ignorance. The current of warm life coursed through his veins like quicksilver. He had imbibed tales of the Madonna, and legends of the saints with his mother's milk. He feared the witches. He was already more skilled in even vague calculations as to winning numbers of the lottery than seemed credible in a sylvan creature, gleaned from listening to the gossip of his elders. Buried treasure, and the signs and symbols leading to its discovery stimulated his most ardent hopes. At least in dreams, or whispering secrets to the other children among the chestnut trees, one dilated on digging in the soil, and coming unexpectedly to a copper pot, filled with jewels, once buried there by brigands. Again, if a lad tended the little black pig in such favoured localities as the Tiber valley, or the Roman Campagna, the useful animal in rooting about could easily turn up a glittering gold coin, a Marengo, for example. Some embryo sentiment of masculine chivalry occasioned the pantomime play of protecting little Egina, the neighbour's daughter, from possible wolves prowling into the chestnut-wood from the heights, on a cold winter day, with much fearsome shouting, capering, and brandishing of a cudgel to frighten off the enemy. Carlo was not as yet touched by the tender passion. He did not bring the gifts of fruit and flowers of the bucolic swain in homage to the ragged and barefooted little Egina. All too soon that young person would put up her hair in an elaborate coiffure, and sigh for feminine finery, while the lad's nature developed under the sway of folly and jealousy of rivals. Tragedy and violence would then be gently condoned by a lenient public as an "affair of love."

A Milanese author states:

"Around the Lake of Como is to be found perhaps the most ingenious and industrious population of Europe. Every portion of these narrow confines has sent forth and maintained colonies of transplanted families. For many years there has not been a shore, or a valley of the lake without natives in Spain, Germany, Portugal, or Sicily. From this nook have emanated machinery, electricity, physical experiments, and the fabrication of such instruments as barometers and telescopes. From the Three Parishes wine merchants and innkeepers have established themselves elsewhere,

A World's Shrine

as well as dealers in silk and linen. Masons and white-washers have formed co-operations, with laws almost republican. . . . The emigration has not been solely from the shores of Larius, but from the border of the Ceresio, and the Valtellina, where every valley has furnished a contingent of stone-cutters, workers in stucco, chimney-sweeps, porters, and game-keepers."

As regards boyhood, Carlo had all the chances of his race. What if a keen *maëstro* on a holiday out from Milan heard the lad singing like a blackbird, and discerned a future tenor or baritone, destined to win fame, in the healthy rustic? What if an artist made an excursion among the hills, with his sketch-book in hand, and found Carlo a clever pupil, as Cimabue discovered Giotto so long ago? Swept away to studio and gallery Carlo might emulate Pietro Ligario of Sondrio, who studied at Rome, Venice, and Milan, and returned to the Valtellina in 1727, where he found slight encouragement for his art, until patronised by the Baron de Salis, and at the close of his career there was scarcely a church of his native province without one of his altar pieces.

Boyhood

Nobody had noted these qualities in Carlo, as yet. He was indolent, mute, uncomprehending of the dormant traits of Shakespeare's youth:

> "True, I talk of dreams,
> Which are the children of an idle brain;
> Begot of nothing but vain fantasy;
> Which is as thin of substance as the air;
> And more inconstant than the wind."

Autumn in all the warmth of resplendent tones of amber, russet, and amethyst brooded in the sunny stillness of noon on Como. The November night had brought a hint of frost to the holly of lower slopes, purple juniper, arbutus, spindle-wood, or scarlet broom. The amphitheatre of hills of the Pian di Tivano glowed with the copse of crimson and yellow bloom, and the bells of a herd of cattle, guarded by shaggy men, were audible on the flanks of Monte San Primo. Masses of rock towered up on all sides, as if chiselled in sharp outline on the sky, and veined with colour as rich in gradation of hues, tawny gold, copper, or grey, as the clinging vines of adjacent vegetation. The oak brushwood formed a zone

A World's Shrine

of golden red. In clefts and crannies of the limestone Pteris Cretica flourished, and spikes of gentian. This Val di Nesso extends to the Pian di Tivano, as does Val Esino from Varenna to the Cainallo Pass, or the Val di Gravedona to the San Jorio Pass.

The boy Carlo hastened to join his companions in the joyous harvest time. The men beat the branches, the children gathered up the chestnuts from the ground, and the women carried them homeward in the baskets on their backs. Such was the hope of each year to the population, with rights of the commune over certain tracts to be respected, and property of families or individuals left untouched, while the poor followed as gleaners.

The chestnut-wood belongs to that upper realm of light, wind, and sunshine. Ah, the dear, beneficent chestnut trees of Italy, France, and Spain that feed so many hungry mouths! The benefactor of the human race who plants a tree must win paradise. How friendly, almost human in protection of shade, are the trunks rising straight

Boyhood

and symmetrical here, and bent or twisted by the storms and years there, if not fallen prone among the mosses, and lichen-covered rocks. A refuge to seek in all emergencies, the wood of Nesso extended the shelter of wide-spreading boughs in rain and heat to childhood, and even the deeper troubles of maturity, for women to sob away grief, soothed by the myriad rippling sounds of swaying foliage, and water, or manhood to wrestle with anger and revenge, and possibly conquer these terrible instincts.

In winter patches of snow lingered in the hollows amidst the dead leaves swept into billows by the storms. Spring decked the glades with green and gold, and gave to the bushes and chestnuts their blossoms, and first tufts of leaves. Then the soft unfolding of summer hours brought the ripened fruit of autumn, and all hearts rejoiced if the harvest was sound and abundant. Ah, the good chestnuts! Young Carlo knew their bounty to the land. Gathered in the wood, they were heaped on mats of cane, and smoke-dried over a fire, then shelled by beating together in a bag, and ground to flour at the mill. How delicious to juvenile hunger the flour mixed with water, spread on dried chestnut-leaves, and baked between two heated stones in the mode of Lucca! Then the polenta, the fritters temptingly fried, and the great cake in a pan, on a three-legged stool, mingled with oil and spices, of a dark chocolate colour, the top powdered with flour, of which delicacy one bought a wedge-shaped slice. Carlo had only heard of these luxuries. The career of the chestnut-roaster, who quits his native canton Ticino with the first cold weather, to set up his little furnace on the street corners of Florence, Rome, or Genoa, and serve the nuts crisp and hot to pedestrians, is an enviable calling.

When the last group had departed, and the early nightfall shrouded the heights, the trees rustled and communed together in their own fashion. A patriarch, gnarled and twisted with years, yet still left standing, with a stanch hold of roots in the soil, remarked to the more vigorous generations, and the saplings ranged about:

Boyhood

"We have given man of our bounty another year. May the good food be blessed to his need. How they grow up, the children. The lad was fetched here in his cradle only the other spring, and he may become one of the old gleaners, in his time, never quitting the shadow of our branches. Who knows?"

The saplings laughed among themselves. They had not yet had their day.

"Time passes, and carries away everything," murmured the patriarch chestnut tree. *Il tempo passa, e porta via ogni cosa.* The generations of visitors come and go through the gates of Como, but the sunset glows on the surface of the waters, and the twilight gathers beneath the cliffs unchanged in the recurring years.

XXV

TRAGEDY IN SUNSHINE

IN the year 1900, July the thirtieth was a Monday, soft, calm, and languid, with all the promise of midsummer heat in the morning hours after a night of storms. The lake world wore its most hushed, and even somnolent aspect of peaceful loveliness. The Como craft passed on the silvery current of the waters in a listless fashion. An early steamer glided from one shore to the other silently. The stranger, pausing in the shade of oleander, acacia, and palm on the bank to watch the black poodle take a bath in the limpid wavelets of the little pebbly beach below, was vaguely aware that these boats had no music and crowd of work-a-day folk from Milan on board, out for a *festa*, but one flag trailing astern at half-mast.

Tragedy in Sunshine

A young nursemaid and a bevy of children were fishing over the stone parapet of the pier, and landed a victim occasionally, with much merriment and splashing, destined for the noonday frying-pan of the household taking the August holiday in an apartment on Como. Suddenly they dropped their fishing-gear, and took flight, like a flock of birds, along the road to meet the father as he slowly approached perusing a morning journal. The group thus passed, the young nursemaid and the children gazing intently at burly Paterfamilias, who read a sentence aloud in a rapid undertone. At least the little ones received an impression of the momentous events of life through their dilated, dark eyes! Possibly the phrases to be current coin in the land were first printed in that morning journal: " after the catastrophe," or " before the disaster."

Then the English officer, just returned from a hospital in South Africa, limped across the path to take his place in the gaily tinted cockle-shell boat, with awning spread, and paused to light his pipe, querying:

A World's Shrine

"You have heard the news? They have killed the king at Monza near here. The townspeople have been gathered about the office of the telegraph all night. Surely we live in evil times!"

How still it was after that! A grey shadow of subtle change to gloom and chill seemed to pass over mountain and lake, so readily does nature lend herself to the mood of humanity in such spots. The steamers glided across to the other shore with their pennants drooping to the tide. A passing breeze lifted the great banner of the hotel on its staff, and swayed the black pennants attached. The poodle emerged from the bath, dripping and wretched, and whimpered unnoticed.

The boatman, tall, supple, and bronzed, averted his face in walking past.

"Boatman! Is it true that the king is dead?"

"It is true, Signore," replied the boatman, touching his cap, yet with eyes steadily turned away.

The gardener, small, sturdy, and good-natured,

Tragedy in Sunshine

who had gossiped with the foreigner for the last half-hour concerning his flower parterres, fetched a basket of shrubbery clippings to cast into the lake.

"Gardener! Have they killed the king?"

"They have killed him, Signore," and the gardener hastened on with an expression of dread of further interrogation.

Such was the awakening of Como on the summer morning. Trifling incidents remain photographed on the mind in the impressions of that day of tragedy in sunshine. The hours dragged on filled with fresh details of events which would become historical, at least in Italy.

The king, arrived once more at Monza, his favourite summer residence of many years, attended the anniversary of the gymnasium of the town. He had witnessed the prowess of vainglorious striplings in the exercises with the affability of his race.

"Ah! When I was young, I was also fond of such feats," he said, in farewell, as he entered his carriage amidst the acclamations of the crowd,

A World's Shrine

the strains of martial music, and the dazzling glow of electric light.

The report of a pistol cut the air with a sinister vibration.

"It is nothing," sighed the brave and honourable gentleman, and fell forward into eternal silence at the gates of his own home.

The royal equipage whirled swiftly under the sheltering trees of the avenue, but Fear flew at greater speed in warning. The queen, in her shining white robes of a State reception, and surrounded by her court, came forth from the palace portal to receive him. A clement monarch, who strove to do his duty, and a noble breast pierced by a cowardly bullet; such remains the record of the July night. The pitiable narration may well inspire in the heart of man surprise, indignation, and sorrow the world over. He must have been ready to resign his sceptre to another hand, for if ever ruler tasted the bitterness of human ingratitude, in manifold phases, it was he. Only that charming surrounding of stanch family loyalty and affection can have sustained him, at times, and rendered enviable his lot, to prince or peasant alike.

The telegraph thrilled with its message to the Duke of Genoa off Naples:

"*Humbert, three times wounded, is dead. Seek Vittorio.*
"MARGHERITA."

In due course "the young man on the sea," came to his right of inheritance. Already the modern Italian poet tunes his lyre to the rendering of this dirge of the storm as unfolding new destinies of the Latin soul. In the shadow of profound grief he dreams that Italy, the ancient, will rise anew, and illumine with her torch the path of unborn heroes.

The July day on Como waned. The moon rose in the pulseless evening hours, fragrant with gardens, and shone far on the tranquil waters until obscured by clouds tinged copper-red, melting to a film of black mist. Superstitious credence in dread portents held dominion over the lake world.

XXVI

THE WINDS OF COMO

MID-WAY on the lake shores a Castle of Indolence stands on a promontory, with spacious chambers and wide-spreading awnings, inviting to repose after the fatigue of oily railway and dusty mountain road. The place is an æolian harp, swept by every wind of Como, wailing down the chimneys at midnight, sighing through half-closed casements in the dawn, and crashing glass doors together ruthlessly in some treacherous gust of noon-day. Pilgrims to the world's shrine pervade these precincts, arriving by the four gates of entrance to the tiny paradise, in search of an atmosphere of indulgent ease, of calmness of mind, of even good-natured lounging, according to the poet, remote from ambition, envy, and strife. They come in cheerful, family

The Winds of Como

groups from the Antipodes, in formidable phalanx of lady travellers personally conducted on summer tours, in throngs of skurrying boy cyclists "doing" the land on a wheel under the guidance of a master tutor. These hosts fill the place to the roof with a transient bustle and animation, and depart leaving the winds once more in possession of deserted corridors.

It were sheer calumny to designate the worthy Swiss porter, who sorts all these human bundles, so to speak, tracks missing feminine travelling-bags, and attends to the bicycles, as the doorkeeper of the original Castle of Indolence, who provided slippered ease for guests, then returned to doze at his post. On the contrary, the modern Swiss inspires the conviction that he is always on duty in his stiff livery, and that he dispenses with sleep altogether in the interest of early train and late steamer, unless he indulges in a brief nap hung on a peg in his little den of an office with his rain cloak.

The pilgrims ebb and flow, and the castle stands forsaken.

A World's Shrine

"Was nought around but images of rest;
Sleep-soothing groves, and quiet lawns between,
And flowery beds that slumbrous influences kest,
From poppies breath'd."

I. THE SOUTH WIND.

At noon of a June day a silvery ripple marks the entrance of Lecco into Como, and the *breva*, or south wind, begins to blow. Is it the most balmy zephyr of earth, filling the square sails of the boats waiting to catch the favourable breeze, and fanning humanity with a pure and soft refreshment of sunny air which permeates all the veins, the very sources of being, with a sort of intoxication after winter fog and spring storm? The mere expansion of living and breathing suffices when the *breva* blows over Lake Como. The divine beauty of the world appeals to the soul in an etherealised and radiant sense. The precious boon of existence questioned by wise and gloomy schools of philosophy of the day, becomes exalted to a pæan of devout thanksgiving and praise to the Creator of worlds in the human breast, as kindred of the birds circling

The Winds of Como

high in the air, the olive trees of the slope, the flowers swaying on their stalks. The psalmist would have here sung of the pleasant pastures and tranquil waters where the kind Shepherd led His poor, foolish sheep for peace.

O Pilgrim! Inhale with full lungs the air to keep always in remembrance the hour! Note the play of light as the ripples sparkle over the current, and the lake reflects the azure hue of the sky for a future time when dark shadows of trouble may gather around your path. Listen to the airy modulations of the music made by the south wind playing pranks through the mansion in contrast with all the blatant discords awaiting you in a return to cities. The moment is valuable, full of sweetness and hope, in the stealing away of wisdom from the degenerate crowd in the effort to soar above the little scene of things.

Who can resist castle-building, with half-shut eyes, when the south wind blows on Como? The pilgrim conjures up, in the waving of a fairy's wand, a castle of indolence on one of the heights, close-hid amidst embowering trees, served by in-

A World's Shrine

visible menials, and more delightful than one of Pliny's villas. Here would he dwell and cast off care, as a garment, far from the world — while the *breva* prevails.

Thus the summer day passes. The native is complacent. The *breva* is not even a fair wind, but only the air of good weather, in popular parlance.

"The wind seems to blow everywhere, yet there is no draught, and one does not catch cold," remarks the wreck of influenza, testing the back of his head with an apprehensive hand, where each hair is standing on end in the gusts waving curtains and flapping awnings.

With the sunset this beneficent current drops to calm. The mortal craft cherishes the souvenir of noon, when the silvery line heralded the advent of the *breva* by the route of Lecco, and the sail of life filled to the breeze and was wafted on the glittering waters of pleasure.

The Winds of Como

II. The Baleful Wind.

The July afternoon is sultry. An aspect of suspense and immobility is manifest in all nature, which is oppressive and menacing. The scent of oleander and jasmine, mingled with dusty honey-bloom, as of clover and cut grass, is heavy and languid. Clouds of a woolly opacity gather slowly about all the mountain peaks, and cling to the slopes in dense masses. The vapours move from the direction of the St. Gothard range, and an occasional hot puff of wind accompanies their advance. It is the breath of the scirocco — damp, enervating, and storm-laden. The hills above Varenna gloom to awful grandeur of black and purple tints in the sullen waiting of the elements. The pilgrim observes these changes almost with bated breath, feeling like a fly at the base of a cliff about to be crushed by a cloud-bolt or granite rock. If the upper world is clothed in majestic sublimity, how can mere language describe the water of the lake? Whence has it borrowed first the wealth of varying hues

A World's Shrine

outspread before the spectator, with the sombre hill sentinels rising above, and the angry swirl of mists obscuring the horizon? All the dying glories of day, quenched elsewhere, seem to linger on Como. The current is sapphire, merging to emerald, opal, gold in the richest blending of tones. The surface has a liquid sheen and lustre. The boats cross through a transparent medium of melting jewels. The sun-god still holds sway. When, indeed, the science of colour-music shall be studied as the science of harmonious sound has been, we may hope to grasp the secret of such beauty.

Hark! Was that thunder? The pilgrim enveloped in waterproof habiliments, guide-book in hand, flees to Milan, or Turin, leaving the baleful wind in possession of the deserted Castle of Indolence, to wail in vestibule and salon, while torrents of rain invade garden paths and strip shrubbery, and scimitars of fire mark the passage of the boats on the pallid stretch of lake.

The Winds of Como

III. THE NIGHT WIND.

Oh, the cool night wind that sweeps down from the Alpine barrier on Como! It is the rival of the *breva* of caressing softness. Turn back from the lake shore in the gloaming, and receive the greeting of the mountain realm. Every cleft and ravine waft their aromatic odours of plant, vine, and blossom in the mingled spicy breath of juniper, thyme, and saxifrage. The face seems pressed against a rocky rampart and buried in ferns. Twilight is here, as in all Italy, Stendhal's hour of the Ave Maria, a moment of pensive meditation and melancholy souvenir. On the high ledges still gleam little hamlets, and a church tower that sends forth a liquid note of evening prayer to be carried far by the night wind. Midnight draws a veil of mystery over the shore, the lapsing waters, and the masses of verdure swathed in shadow. Dull oblivion of repose in closed chambers is sinful if only the Pilgrims, as children of a larger growth, can prop their eyelids open and keep awake to enjoy the miracles of

A World's Shrine

change of the Southern night. Oh, sweet and pure wind, where did you first spread your wings to start forth over glacier slope, through mossy dell, and down the giddy plunge of foaming cascades on your nocturnal rambles? Imagination runs riot in the darkness, full of fleeting shapes, taking form and vanishing amidst the swaying branches and foliage. If one could be metamorphosed by the witchery of night into one of the feline tribe, and prowl, sure-footed, along the crags overhanging precipices, with eyes of green fire capable of piercing obscurity to the depths, and a sense of hearing so fine and alert for sound of danger, or lurking foe, that the ears of mankind, in comparison, might be likened to the handles of coarse jugs, fashioned by Phœnician or Aztec potters! To feel the glory of strength, and suppleness of movement of the animal kingdom, and roam among the mountains is an instinct born of the night wind rustling the roses and laurel of the terrace, and sobbing insistently beneath the eaves of the Castle of Indolence. As the hours wear on if the stupid pilgrim must doze,

MENAGGIO

The Winds of Como

at least step out on the balcony at dawn. A crescent of golden, waning moon hangs in the sky, the lake below is a crystal shield, and beyond the opposite peaks a rose-pink flush deepens. The wind is lulled to stillness.

The first man who visited the spot flits again along the heights. He is a vision, a mere conjecture in the great human family. What manner of creature was he? An artist has depicted the last man standing on the world. The study is majestic, even awe-inspiring. Fain would we catch the image of the first man who gazed on Como through the veil of dim tradition, and early fable. Did he come merely as a tourist? According to Sir John Lubbock the love of travel is deeply implanted in the human breast. He surely was furnished with no other guide-book than his own eye and ear. Was he induced to settle in the delightful locality? There can be no doubt of his great antiquity. Baron Bunsen claims the age on the earth of the highest race as twenty thousand years. Switzerland is stated to have been inhabited by man for six or seven

A World's Shrine

thousand years. The biologist and the geologist may place the finger of science on our hero, with a chuckle of triumph. As we seek him through that fog of vague surmise in the spring morning he was a troglodyte, a hunter, a herdsman, a fisherman, and even a rudimentary agriculturist. He is supposed to have early availed himself of the quarry of soft stone in the Val Bregaglia, known in Pliny's day, to fashion the soup-pot and platters of his hearth. Was he Gaul, Rhetian, Teuton, this vigorous figure full of a mysterious significance in the succeeding tide of movement of tribes and nations? He was a pioneer of the holiday pilgrims now flocking through the four gates of this exotic garden. He carved the bone with strange device of ornamentation, shaped the flint with cunning hand, and split the rebel rock by dint of effort, until a spark of fire flashed from the stone by which he made the world his own. Possibly he dwelt, at some period, on a shallow reach of the lake in a hut of planks supported on piles, and connected by a bridge with the land, lowering a basket through a trap-door to catch

The Winds of Como

the fish which furnished his food, as well as the Swiss Lake inhabitants, and those of Lake Garda; early architecture imitated by the City of Tcherkask on the Don, and the Dyaks of Borneo. He was as free as air in that primeval existence, with all the instincts of his being keenly alert in self-preservation. As a hunter he rifled the eagle's nest of the crags, ranged the forest, and slew the wolf, badger, marmot, hare, and otter of the lake, with arrow and spear, to devour their flesh, and clothe himself in their skins. The bear was his lawful prey, as bruin is still of the son of the Grisons, who nails skull and paws, as a trophy, above the door of his chalet. As a herdsman he was shaggy and robust, like his descendants of the hills of the *Pian di Tivano*. His habitation was scarcely more than the hut of reeds, bound together with ropes of the Roman Campagna, a bed of boards covered with skins, a few cooking utensils, and a milk pail. The religion of that early time was the worship of the Gods of rocks, trees, and mountains. His daughter, the young girl who kept alive the flame on the hearth, kindled from

A World's Shrine

sparks of flint, or two sticks rubbed together, while father and brothers hunted, or fished, was the prototype of the Vestal Virgin in guarding the symbolical sacred flame of the Palladium.

Thus life, through those earlier elements, has flowed on.

In the morning mists the Bergamo shepherd folk, hardy, bronzed, and frugal, making ready to scale the Maloja Pass with their flocks in quest of summer herbage, probably resemble that first man, the common ancestor of the region.

The son of the soil, the husbandman, pausing under a fig-tree, *falcetto*, or pruning-hook, in hand, and contemplating his sphere of labour amidst the vines, olives, and mulberries of the terraces, is his grandson. The fog melts to gauze, and softly drifts away. The peasant resumes his toil where the bean harvest bursts the shattered pod, light vetch, and bitter lupin grow. He knows, with Cicero, that he plants a tree not one berry of which he will ever gather. He is further aware that:

> "Never will the earth unaided
> Yield the ripe, nutritious barley."

The Winds of Como

He has risen before the sun to begin his routine of work, to drink the water of his own well, and subsist on the fruits of his own fields. With the nightfall he will seek heavy and weariful slumber. His song through the sultry hours is to query of fate what he has to gain, or to lose by the power of emperors and kings.

IV. THE NORTH WIND.

The north wind is an unwelcome visitor. It pounces on the summer zone as a fierce foe sure of its prey, roughening the water to white-caps so that small craft hug the inlets, parching the soil, and withering the flowers, unless refreshed by continuous jets of spray from hose, and sprinkling-pot. The effect on nerves is vaguely irritating. Acute wakefulness was sure to haunt the pillow of the pilgrim the previous night. Como shakes the head of disapproval. The north wind emanates from the melting snows of the Engadine, and blights exotic vegetation. It is annoying and wearisome, as it mocks at screens and portières, and watches an opportune moment

A World's Shrine

to upset easel table, mirrors, and vases with rude, exuberant hilarity.

Seek a sheltered nook between arbour draped by convolvulus, and a group of evergreen shrubs, and study the upper ranges of space visible through the foliage. Behold mountain and sky in all their remoteness of a clear atmosphere. Pinnacles of scarped stone, worn by storms and time, cut the deep, porcelain blue of the heavens in serrated outline of bold relief, with glistening threads of rills descending here and there, and masses of amethyst crags piled in an amphitheatre in the direction of Colico and the Splügen. These mute guardians of the portals of the lake world imbue the spirit of the wayfarer with indefinable longing of aspiration:

> "He who ascends to mountain-tops shall find
> The loftiest peaks most wrapt in clouds and snow;
> He who surpasses, or subdues mankind
> Must look down on the hate of those below."

The clouds reign above, moving in soft masses of fleecy vapour. Aristophanes might again describe them on this spot to-day:

The Winds of Como

"We dominate the earth, we show our faces to man in changing every instant, yet last to eternity! We spring forth from the bosom of our father the ocean! We climb the snowy summits of the mountains without losing breath, and, suspending ourselves at these heights, we watch our reflection in the azure waters below. If we cease to listen to the solemn murmur of the waves we begin to hear the subdued harmonies of divine rivers. Our rôle is marvellous! Have we not received from Jupiter the mission to make sparkle in the eyes of men the riches of the firmament? Does not our light envelope separate the living world from cold, unpitying, eternal death?"

The atmosphere embraces all, bathes, fills, composes the forest tree, the grass, and grain of the field, the fruits of these shores, almond, orange, grape of the vine. Nay! Is not the very soul of man clothed with air?

The winds of Como are played on the instrument of hill and dale, and the pilgrims to a world's shrine come and go with new generations.

CPSIA information can be obtained
at www.ICGtesting.com
Printed in the USA
LVOW03*1104070716
495467LV00010B/47/P